# UNCONDITIONALLY

## FINDING JESUS IN THE EUCHARIST

### BY: GREG WASINSKI

# UNCONDITIONALLY
## Finding Jesus in the Eucharist

Cover Design by Frank J. Wasinski III

Printed in the United States of America

ISBN: 978-0-9860269-2-8

Learn more at: www.GregWasinski.com

GREG WASINSKI

*For my wife, Aimee.*

*Thank you for always being my "home"
and helping me once again find Jesus through you.*

# CONTENTS

# PREFACE

---

*"If angels could be jealous of men, they would be so for one reason: Holy Communion." ~St. Maximilian Kolbe*

---

My professor in college, Dr. Michael Barber, once said, "Everyone wants to go to Heaven, but no one wants to die." How true it is. But what if I told you that you didn't have to die in order to hold Heaven in your hands? All you need to do is visit the Eucharist and the Angels will surround you as the One who rules the Heavens and the Earth fills you with everything your heart longs to experience. Heaven in your midst.

As a lifelong Catholic I spent many years going through the motions of mass, catechism class, Sacramental preparation and prayer without allowing myself to appreciate the beauty of our faith. During an adult period of my life, I even drifted away from going to church all together. So often, even when I was present, I had zero realization or respect of the Real

1

Presence of Jesus Christ in the Eucharist. I allowed myself to be disconnected. I didn't have the desire to encounter Him and accept His unconditional love found through His sacrifice and resurrection in the Eucharist. I didn't appreciate the gift before me in the person of our Savior.

There weren't hundreds of changes I needed to make in my life in order to find Jesus in the Eucharist. I didn't have to go back to school, nor did I need to memorize specific scripture verses. I needed to allow Christ into places of myself I was never willing to before. I had to be brave enough to surrender everything I was holding back in my heart from God. By offering myself, I became aware how much He was offering me. I began to feel His presence and then allow everything He was, and is, to consume every part of me from the moment I received Holy Communion.

We can walk away from a lot of things in religion. Even dismiss the everyday faith and real life moments which occur in the world around us. However, we cannot deny the moment we feel our heart come alive because we have found all of Christ in the Supper of the Lord. If we begin to accept how deeply He wants to give Himself unconditionally over and over in this Sacrament, no matter what happens or where we have been, nothing will ever be able to tear us away from our Catholic faith. No longer will we sit in the pew watching others receive Jesus in the Eucharist because we allowed our sins to prevent us from going to Communion rather than taking the time to be made worthy to receive Him through reconciliation.

This book is an invitation. A note from the Bridegroom, asking you to once again connect with Him or to receive Him for the first time in your life. This is an open request to allow yourself to live with a child-like faith that not only calls you into a deeper relationship with the Lord, but one that allows you to see yourself as He does: loved unconditionally.

Put away any misnomers that prevent you from falling deeply in love with the beauty of this sacrifice and open your heart; absorb all He is offering to you through the Eucharist. See Him for what He is, truly present, calling to you, to give all of Himself. He loves you that much. He only longs for you to simply say "yes" with your "Amen" to show you love Him as unconditionally in return.

# PROLOGUE

You're sitting in mass, praying and going through the motions of a normal Sunday obligation. You've taken your usual spot in your favorite row. Amidst the children crying, the occasional cell phone going off and someone around you being ahead of all the prayers by one or two words, it seems to be a typical liturgy. You have gathered a few things from the homily, which inspire you, and a quick glance at your watch reassures you that Father is on schedule with the allotted time you determined in your head.

As the Mass has now reached the offertory of gifts, your mind wonders a bit because there's really nothing in it for you at this point. However, you happen to know the family who has been chosen to bring them to the altar and you chuckle as they hand the gifts off before they awkwardly look at one another not knowing whether to talk to the priest, bow or just turn around and walk back to their seats. You then hear the last note of the offertory song end and involuntarily your body cues you for the next moment of standing within our "Catholic Calisthenics" of stand, sit, stand, sit, repeat. What you don't know is, in this moment, your faith life is about to change forever and you will never be the same again.

As you look toward the altar, your eyes pan up away from the presider and immediately become glued to the crucifix in the church. The once glazed over "piece of art" has begun to transform from a simple rendition of the crucifixion into something much more. You become transfixed as you see the grain of the wood beginning to show more definition. Splinters, knots and imperfections appear.

The once perfect ninety-degree angled shape of the cross no longer has its crisp straight edges the artist intended. Despite being in shock at the intersected wooden beams this backdrop has become, you are in utter disbelief to witness what happens next. The once hand crafted depiction of Christ is now taking on flesh. It prominently displays the cuts, bruises and welts of the real body of our Lord and Savior as it was on Good Friday. At the completion of this transformation, He now hangs in front of you on the cross as if it was the day He was crucified thousands of years ago. He is limp, broken beyond repair, yet there is peace within His, now at rest, body. In amazement, you feel as if someone has sucked all the air from your lungs. While you stare motionless, the sound in the church has become different; even white noise ceases to exist.

The priest continues with the Mass, now reaching the Eucharist prayers. In amazement, your heart races, you frantically rub your eyes. You desperately look around the church to see if anyone else is seeing what your entire being is entranced by. Yet, no one seems to have the same astonished look on their face you feel that you do. Once more, rubbing your eyes even more forcefully, you look back to the cross to see if all this was merely the work of a daydream. It's not. He remains in front of you as real as ever. You are not sure whether to faint, cry out or weep, however one thing is for sure, the Lord is present in your midst.

In the moments of time, which have seemed to stand still, the Mass continues on, now reaching the moment for Holy Communion. Sweat begins to drip from your brow and chills fill your entire being. The Eucharistic Ministers have gathered around the sanctuary and each person has taken their place for "business as usual" in the distribution of the Sacrament. Tears fill your eyes as you are immersed at what you see in front of you. Every hair on your body seems to be on end and your insides tingle as you want to scream out, "Doesn't anyone else see that He is here? Jesus is right in front of us!"

Seconds now seem like hours and minutes feel like days. You await the usher to call your row, which seems to take a lifetime. You need to walk down the aisle and get an even closer look. Marching forward, hands folded, it's impossible to take your eyes off the surreal image of Christ hanging on the cross in front of you. Small droplets of blood begin to trickle down His arms till they gently roll to His fingertips to the ground below forming tiny pools. You have never felt this close to the Lord. As you shuffle toward the priest, waiting your turn, you intently look at each person receiving the Eucharist.

Not wanting your moment to end in seeing this magnificent image before you, you gaze adoringly. Your heart desires only to lay at His feet and sob. What radiates from the cross could not ever be put into words. Your soul jumps, making you long for all He is, nothing can stop you from getting to Him. There is nothing between you and the Eucharist but a few steps. Just then, a ladder is put in place at the foot of the cross. You are next to receive communion. Joyfully, the priest gazes in your eyes, smiles widely, and turns to the side to look back toward the crucifix; he knows what you see and what your soul can no longer live without.

You both watch as a plainly dressed man with nothing more than a tool belt around his waist climbs up the ladder near the crucifix. He pulls out a hammer and using the claw portion, he works with great might to remove the nails, first from Christ's left wrist. In that instant you see Jesus' body slump a little lower than it was before; you want to run to Him but your legs won't cooperate.

Next, the worker removes the nails from His feet and His right hand which results in the Lord falling into the man's arms. Gently and caringly, he brings Jesus down from the cross. The priest walks to the man and lovingly takes Jesus from him, coddling Him in his arms like a mother would hold a child who has been injured. Father walks back to you, your heart feels like it might explode and air still cannot fill your lungs. How is it possible that you are this close to everything you have ever believed? In the next moment the priest says those words you have heard a thousand times before, "The Body of Christ," then places Jesus in your outstretched arms.

His skin is tender, He is frail, and His face, although tired from the struggle of His sacrifice, is filled with a grace, which consumes your heart. Stunned, but in love, you slowly walk back with Him to your pew, tears steaming, holding Him, thanking Him, and understanding what every sacrifice he endured for you meant.

Others in the church who have experienced what you are currently living, smile proudly as you make your way back to your seat. You are in awe, submersing yourself in the greatest gift you could receive. How could it be possible to have Jesus Christ in your midst to reassure you of the faith you have held for so long but never realized the true beauty of your faith? You never want to leave this moment. Nothing in the world matters, having Jesus in your arms takes away every anxiety and fear, replacing them with hope and reassurance. You remain in your pew while the world has stopped, repeating over and over a combination of thanksgiving, contrition and praise to the Lord. Nothing else in the world exists but you and Him.

When we allow ourselves to be united with Christ in the way He intended in the Eucharist, we no longer have to imagine the scenario above. What if for one moment each of us had an experience like this during Mass, a moment where Christ comes to us in a new way to love us unconditionally. Never in a million years could we look at the beautiful gift of the Eucharist the same, much less, think about taking communion and walk out the doors to our car. Never could we go back to our seats after receiving Him, only to think about what we will do after Mass, letting our minds wander off instead of falling into prayer.

Truth is, this is exactly what happens every time we walk up to receive Holy Communion. Not only do we receive the Body and Blood of Christ, we receive everything that Jesus was, is and ever shall be. As St. Thomas Aquinas boldly states, "The actual effect of the Eucharist is the transformation of man into God."

We must never again see the Eucharist "host" as merely a wafer, a symbol or "Jesus for a moment." Rather we must remember that by finding Jesus in the Eucharist, it is the real presence of love, forgiveness, strength, courage and every other attribute, which Christ enveloped. How lucky we are for the gift of the Lord's Supper and being even closer to Him than the disciples were.

I pray we never again look at Holy Communion as simply an act or just part of the Mass we do each week or in some cases once a year. Rather, it's the relationship we desire which centers us to know what we believe as Catholic Christians is true. It could be the one missing link our soul is starving for and our heart needs in order to find fulfillment in faith, religion and life all together. Once each of us appreciates the Eucharist in this way, nothing will ever tear us away from the beauty of the Catholic faith, nor cannot it keep us away from making Mass the priority it should be. One thing is for certain, if we continually find Jesus in the Eucharist through His real presence, these moments will happen, maybe not with our eyes, but throughout our entire being any time we have the opportunity to invite Him to become part of us.

# INTRODUCTION

---

*"If we really understood the Mass, we would die of joy." ~St. John Vianney*

---

Author Brennan Manning once said, "My deepest awareness of myself is that I am deeply loved by Jesus Christ and I have done nothing to earn it or deserve it." I think many of us have felt like that one way or another in our lives. Possibly, some of us have never even thought about our relationship with Him in this manner. Still, the Lord comes to us unconditionally so that we may return to him in the same way. No strings attached. The complete giving of Himself without reservation means we cannot place conditions on our relationship with Him. Specifically, how we will commit to worship him, receive Him in the Eucharist or work to be an authentic disciple within the church community which represents His love. We will continually struggle without fully acknowledging our need for a personal connection with Jesus Christ; not just the human person, but the Divine being who brings all of His works, love and mercy into our hearts when we consume Him in the Eucharist.

Finding Jesus in the Eucharist consists of everything that we think we see but really cannot fully comprehend till we reflect on what is being offered. We simply see a cup or bowl that holds wine and a wafer. What's beyond that appearance is the actual life and works of Christ that are poured into us each time we feast on, and with, Him. To say we consume "Him," means we consume ALL of Him. We immediately find Him through everything He experienced; moments of prayer, learning, leading, sacrifice, compassion, service and all of the things which made Jesus whole. By receiving Holy Communion, we accept His open invitation to dine with Him in order to allow Christ to become completely one with us. To find Jesus in the Eucharist, is to see Him beyond the sacrament, uniting believers who become the church through this communion. We even share a spiritual communion with those who simply stare into His eyes through the act of Adoration, listening fervently for His voice to answer their deepest hidden prayers.

As Catholics, our fundamental principal of the Eucharist is that Christ is fully present in His body and His blood right in front of us. Not a symbol, not just a ceremony within our tradition. No, it's Jesus Christ, our Savior and our hope, presenting Himself once again.

Our world offers many denominations of Christianity which allow us to form a relationship with Jesus Christ. The one thing that is missing in this encounter with Him created specifically through His continual sacrifice and resurrection in the Eucharist. A chance to spend each day with Him inside of us renewing our being, sharing the Last Supper with Him just as the disciples did. He desires for us to take the time to allow Him to simply be part of us.

*"Those who receive the Eucharist are united more closely to Christ. Through it Christ unites them to all the faithful in one body - the Church." (Catechism of the Catholic Church 1396)*

If we become the church when we consume the Eucharist, then the real answer in finding Him is that we need not look any further than ourselves. It becomes a tremendous responsibility when we are called to be Christ; one that sometimes feels to be too much. But why? If we desire to have a God who loves us unconditionally and shepherds us on the road which leads to the fulfillment of life through His sacrifice, then what would make our role within the flock any different for us to become that model of God? We are a living vessel that offers the same image to others. It's how we conduct ourselves which reflects His love into others through self-sacrifice and belief which ultimately leads others to join the journey with us. Basically, it is in giving that not only do we receive His grace but we feel compelled to share it with the world.

How deep is the faith we find through the Eucharist? Nearly every Apostle died for it, people around the world today are still persecuted for it and those who make an effort to live out their faith are challenged at some point by someone who chooses not to believe. Within all of that is the very hope and knowledge that what we find in a relationship with Christ is fulfillment. Daily encounters and life experiences where Christ is present provide a feeling of euphoria so great that we are willing to be discounted by some for believing in the unseen. This is grace, the mystical blessing flowing directly from God into us through the Eucharist. If we never felt His presence with us, then we could not fight for what we believe because we would be empty; nothing to sustain us other than words on the page of a book or host held to the heavens. However, that is not what happens at all. Finding Jesus in the Eucharist creates a gateway in which every ounce of spiritual knowledge flows into us, connecting our beings with the Mystery of Faith. When this happens, we walk away with God inside of us feeling things we never have felt before.

To believe, but still doubt the real presence of Christ in the Eucharist places limitations on the almighty power of God who created all things. The Eucharist is just another amazing gift from our Father, through His Son, to prove nothing is impossible with Him. We pray, we believe, we acknowledge Christ's dying on the cross for us and the Last Supper which preceded it, but when faced with an opportunity to dine at His Eucharistic feast, some question the manner in which he presents Himself with a seed of doubt that possibly it is just a symbol. Why would He go through everything for us just to be a symbol?

This book is not meant to be solely educational, purely theological, nor should it be labeled as "Catholic self-help." It is nearly impossible to scratch the surface of how "all-encompassing" the Eucharist is. All I can do is jump start the journey. Everything written is an invitation to fall in love more deeply. A chance to surrender unconditionally to the One who can give you everything your heart longs for but the world cannot provide. Finding Jesus in the Eucharist isn't a journey just to change how you see the sacrament, it's an encounter to completely transform everything you become when you receive Him, loving Him as unconditionally as He loves you.

# USING THIS BOOK

Outside of the chapter writings, I have offered a few aids to help widen your vision for the journey to find Jesus in the Eucharist. You will notice four specific areas.

## SAINT QUOTES:

There is no better way to continue the tradition of our faith other than to find inspiration from those who were able to connect with Christ so intently during their time on Earth. These quotes start of each chapter and offer beautiful insight on the gifts found in the Eucharist.

## SHARING THE JOURNEY:

These short paragraphs are directly from my own personal Adoration journal. It was important to give you a behind the scenes look of what God has shared with me during our special time, so you can see we all journey together. Let it be the inspiration to record what He is telling you in and out of mass.

## PRAYER:

These prayers relating to the content of the chapter they follow were written by me specifically for this book. I hope they help you to find Jesus in new ways through the Eucharist by praying with them and adding your own touches.

## REFLECTION:

The space is yours do with it as you wish. Jot down what you might have heard within the chapter, write about someone you are praying for, or simply take it to Adoration and journal your insights. But, most of all, use it!

# FINDING JESUS
# IN THE EUCHARIST

# I

# A CALL HOME
## RETURNING TO JESUS IN THE EUCHARIST

---

*"When you approach the tabernacle
remember that he has been waiting for you
for twenty centuries."*
*--St. Josemaria Escriva*

---

When the disciples wanted to find Jesus after the crucifixion they decided to run to the tomb in which He laid. A tomb which was the resting place after the violence of Good Friday, but it held the One who transformed their lives forever; their teacher, friend and Lord. They didn't really expect or understand all Christ foretold about being raised up, they just knew they wanted to be next to Him at all costs. Where do we run when we feel empty? Where do we desire to be, and who do we desire to be with? In the end, we want to be "home," a feeling of peace, security and love. Feelings that at certain times nothing on Earth can provide.

Let's start off by identifying what "home" really is. It's not a place, it's not a destination, it truly is a feeling. Take marriage, or any loving relationship for that matter, as an example. Whether the world is crashing down around you or you're on top of world celebrating life's victories, there's an indescribable feeling being with the person you feel completely safe with. It might be a friend, a sibling, a parent or even a place where you feel something different than with anyone or anything else. Truth is, we can experience the feeling of home regardless of the location where we are; it's not merely defined as the house in which we reside.

Think about the hometown you grew up in and how it makes you feel when you go back. People know you, they make you feel relaxed and their joy to see you is unconditional. Possibly, you might think about a time where strangers gave you a welcome in an unfamiliar place which filled you with an emotion you could not put into words. You felt like they had known you for years which bonded you through instantaneous friendship. These are the factors which allow us to understand how "home" is not the physical place, but rather it's the experience your soul feels to be completely at ease.

Home really is where your heart is and the only One who can truly say where your heart belongs is the Creator who made you in His likeness. The Catechism of the Catholic Church tells us *"God thirsts for us so we may thirst for Him."* (CCC 2560) What better way to quench that thirst than every time we celebrate in partaking in His son who was offered for each and every one of us, regardless of who we think we are or where we have been.

The first question we need to ask ourselves at some point in our faith journey is, "Why do we believe what we believe?"

There is so much which we don't understand and sometimes the world is persuading us to give up on what we believe because there is not "scientific" or full historical proof to every facet of our religion. It's interesting why this is such a hard question because we have no problem identifying ourselves as Catholic, even if we preface if it with, "I am not practicing, I grew up Catholic," or even "I love my faith but I don't agree with _____ (insert issue of the day)."

In the end, we associate ourselves with Catholicism because something inside of us lets us know that it's indeed "home." Whether we always feel that way or not is a different story, but it's really our heart which guides us in our decisions at the end of the day. To be loved unconditionally in the Eucharist fulfills every aspect our soul needs in order to return to God who made us for eternal happiness which we experience when our final end is met.

> "The desire for God is written in the human heart, because man is created by God and for God; and God never ceases to draw man to himself. Only in God will he find the truth and happiness he never stops searching for." (CCC 27)

Then why wouldn't we expect to feel home anytime we are able to invite Christ into our being through the celebration of the Eucharist?

A parable which is used quite frequently in Catholic teaching and evangelization is the story of the Prodigal Son (Lk 15:11-32)

> "I shall get up and go to my father and I shall say to him, "Father, I have sinned against heaven and against you. I no longer deserve to be called your son; treat me as you

*would treat one of your hired workers.'" So he got up and went back to his father. While he was still a long way off, his father caught sight of him, and was filled with compassion. He ran to his son, embraced him and kissed him. His son said to him, 'Father, I have sinned against heaven and against you; I no longer deserve to be called your son.' But his father ordered his servants, 'Quickly bring the finest robe and put it on him; put a ring on his finger and sandals on his feet. Take the fattened calf and slaughter it. Then let us celebrate with a feast, because this son of mine was dead, and has come to life again; he was lost, and has been found.' Then the celebration began." (Lk 15:18-24)*

When preached about, it usually correlates a message meant for all of us. To know the Father is always waiting for our presence no matter where we have been or how long we have been away. What I love to focus on is the fact that the father actually goes out to meet the son before he returns ALL the way home. Some say this is because of jubilation, however there can be an aspect of his action which helps us to understand where Christ meets us in the Eucharist. When the father chooses to go out to see the son returning home, I see it as an act of unconditional love to make sure his son returns all the way back to him.

The son is broken and empty, he is also weak; a weakness which could rob him of the courage it takes to make the final portion of the journey in order to return home safely. Rather than letting anxiety or fear take over as the son gets closer, the father makes sure his return will be complete by meeting him and walking with him the rest of the way. In the same manner, our Father meets us in the Eucharist through Christ to become part of us so we don't have to journey alone. He knows how many times people have made the first step to come home to be with Him, only to have the fear of rejection or a perceived lack of acceptance stop them from completing the journey.

As we take those steps toward Him down the aisle we are coming to receive the Bridegroom who offered us everything we ever wanted and all we have to do is say "yes" in our "Amen." It is the feast which parallels the same one when the son makes it home and his father places his ring on his finger. A feast for a self-deemed "unworthy" son who is nothing less than beautiful in his father's eyes. A father who just wanted his son home by any means necessary. Today, we are the son.

Making the decision to come home to the Father through Jesus in the Eucharist isn't always because we were physically absent. Yes, we have a large population of those who identify themselves with the faith, but of those who participate in mass, there is a larger contingency who have not allowed themselves to be present spiritually. It is impossible to encounter the Lord if we have not given over everything within us to ultimately be at peace and embrace the loving aspects of home experienced through our faith.

Think about every holiday you've had when all the members of your family gathered, but the party took on a life of its own apart from the reason you were getting together. There you all are, Uncle Johnny sleeping on the couch, mom stuck in the kitchen doing dishes, a conversation between two siblings in another room disagreeing on life issues and you, sitting in a recliner staring at the TV not feeling like it's a special occasion at all. Sure the family pictures on the wall remind you of where you belong, but within you, it's only when everyone is present with joy, laughter and an interest in one another when you truly feel home. Church for us is the same way. Especially if we have forgotten about the real reason we are there.

God just doesn't want us in the house, He wants us to be mentally present sharing ourselves with Him so he may share Himself with us. We enter church to come home again. Sinners who need to be loved by the Father. We long to reconnect with our Lord. If we don't allow our heart to find Him, we cannot feel the peace we seek because the encounter with Christ never truly takes place. Our opportunity to reconnect in these precious moments slip away. As the dinner table is set and we join together for food and fellowship, we are reminded of the importance of this special time together as family and the love we share. The Eucharist is our moment as Catholic Christians in the Mass where we find Jesus serving us just as He did with His disciples at the Last Supper to give us the same experience to feel how much we are loved. A gathering in which time stands still and home is felt within the depths of our soul.

The call home for each of us will come in different forms. It just doesn't occur when we are gone, when we are broken or when we feel like we have nowhere left to turn. The home found in Jesus through the Eucharist is offered daily for us to celebrate with Him despite our shortcomings and amidst our celebrations. He is desperately calling you to come home every opportunity you get to remind you of the family to which you belong. To share an intimacy which shows how much He loves you unconditionally. As C.S Lewis so beautifully puts it, "The fact that our heart yearns for something Earth can't supply is proof that Heaven must be our home." Where else can we go to receive His real presence and taste Heaven through the sacrifice Jesus Christ offered for us? Run to Him, His embrace can change you forever.

# SHARING THE JOURNEY:

*Lord it has been so long since I have sat with you, open to your word and strong enough to take it all in. My own weakness is the only thing that helps me from you. Fear, anger, sadness and jealousy are the forces which create a separation of your love and presence*

*I blink and you are there just like your always there, I focused away for a moment and you prove to me that regardless you are right in front of me. I should pay homage at all times because your presence is never ending.*

# PRAYER:

*Heavenly Father, please meet me where I am on my faith journey. I long to know you and experience you more deeply through the beauty of your Son in the Eucharist. Remove all fear and doubt within my heart so I may return to your loving arms always despite where I have been.*

# REFLECTION

_____

_____

_____

_____

_____

_____

_____

_____

_____

_____

_____

_____

_____

_____

_____

# II

# LORD I'M NOT WORTHY
## SEEING OURSELVES AS HE SEES US

---

*"When you look at the Crucifix, you understand how much Jesus loved you then. When you look at the Sacred Host you understand how much Jesus loves you now" ~Mother Teresa*

---

As I mentioned in the outset of the introduction, during particular moments of our faith life there are times we don't feel worthy of the love God has for us. This can actually begin to take shape in a myriad of ways, but usually it will culminate in us running from God instead of to Him. It's why the prayer we offer as we are about to surrender ourselves to be open enough to receive Christ in the Eucharist is even more definitive than we think. I am referring to the words, "Lord I am not worthy to receive you under my roof, but only say the words and my soul shall be healed."

Now for Catholics, prior to the year 2011 the words were a bit different before the Roman Missal changes were adopted. We used to simply say, "Lord I am not worthy to receive you, only say the word and I shall be healed." However, the beauty of the change in this instance, and many other changes within the church, was to go back to literal interpretation of how the "story of salvation" is revealed in scripture. The prayer itself is actually taken from the words the Centurion speaks to Jesus as he pleads for Him to heal the servant back at his home near death. "Lord, I am not worthy for You to come under my roof, but just say the word, and my servant will be healed." (Mt 8:8)

Why is this so important for us to understand? Because the Centurion struggled with his role in the army and how it would look in front of his people by showing belief in Jesus so deeply that he would ask Christ for help. For us, just like the Centurion, we are faced with battles daily of serving the world and at the same time surrendering ourselves to what we know is truth. In our darkest moments, or even just in the battle scars that appear in everyday life, we need to make the invitation for Christ to come into our hearts to dwell, despite the fact we do not feel like a worthy host. By speaking this phrase, we are pleading with the Lord to heal our souls at the center of our being. Sin which enters through our choices, makes us feel that we are less than valuable in God's eyes. This is part of the huge lie the evil one wants us to believe when choices we've made are outside what we believe. The truth is in the beauty unveiled in finding Jesus in the Eucharist just as the Centurion found Him during His travels.

The Father's unconditional love seeks the invitation for us to be willing to host Him in the very place our being dwells: within our soul.

> Because it is the memorial of Christ's Passover, the Eucharist is also a sacrifice. The sacrificial character of the Eucharist is manifested in the very words of institution: 'This is my body which is given for you' and 'This cup which is poured out for you is the New Covenant in my blood.' In the Eucharist Christ gives us the very body which he gave up for us on the cross, the very blood which he 'poured out for many for the forgiveness of sins.' (CCC 1365)

As we speak the words, "Lord I am not worthy," at Mass, it is an admission that while we hold faults deep within, there is only One who can come into our dwelling to make things new again; we just need to invite him.

In the Bible, we never see Christ asking people if they are "worthy" of His love, nor would we ever be witness to Jesus ever telling anyone they are unworthy of His presence. It's the human fear evident in various scripture contexts we read about, from Zaccheus being unwilling to come down from the tree to Dismas' (The Good Thief) final discussion with Christ on the cross. They felt "unworthy," but Jesus saw them differently.

In the case of the good thief, the request of being worthy of Christ's love gives us the ultimate examples of what receiving His love in our life means. This is apparent through his choice of words while being crucified alongside our Savior as written in Luke 23:42, "*Jesus remember me when you come in to your kingdom.*" Jesus' response is simple, "*I assure you, today you will be with me in paradise.*" (Luke 23:43) Now prior to that exchange, the thief acknowledged that his own sentence was just. Meaning he had broken the law of the land in some manner. During his final confession, he revealed that he had not lived a proper life to get into heaven. However, Christ was not seeking whether or not Dismas thought he was worthy of the Kingdom of God, but showed how unconditionally Christ's saving power is by re-assuring him they would be together forever in the promise of heaven despite the thief's past.

We place ourselves before the Lord to find salvation in the Eucharist, receiving all of Him into our core, with all certainty He is present. His promise is the same for all of us. Allowing Him to be king to share Himself with us grants us the same assurance of paradise as the "good thief." When we have welcomed our own cross, allowing ourselves to die to an old life with the promise of a better one as a believer in all Christ gives us unconditionally, He makes us worthy for our eternal home with the Father.

Now in both cases, of the Centurion and the "good thief," we can find ourselves wanting to hear more of their story. We want to know how things went once they actually accepted the Lord's invitation to dine with Him literally and figuratively. Since it is not recorded in the bible, let's turn to another example of a man who felt unforgivable and at times, distant from Christ; Peter, the Apostle, the "Rock of the Church." Their relationship allows us to see how deeply Christ's conviction overshadows a person's "worthiness" to not only remain loved, but to continue nurturing them on the path they have been called into by the Lord.

The instance with Peter we focus on to show how Christ accepts us in order to fully accept His love, is after Peter denied Christ three times during the journey to the cross. Jesus had already risen from the dead and was now appearing a third time to the disciples to fulfill all He had foretold those who would carry on His church. In John 21:15-17, Jesus is on the shore with Peter and Jesus is inquiring how deeply Peter is able to love his Master.

> "When they had finished breakfast, Jesus said to Simon Peter, "Simon, son of John, do you love me more than these?"* He said to him, "Yes, Lord, you know that I love you." He said to him, "Feed my lambs." He then said to him a second time, "Simon, son of John, do you love me?" He said to him, "Yes, Lord, you know that I love you." He said to him, "Tend my sheep." He said to him the third time, "Simon, son of John, do you love me?" Peter was distressed that he had said to him a third time, "Do you love me?" and he said to him, "Lord, you know everything; you know that I love you." [Jesus] said to him, "Feed my sheep."

It's important to point out that just a few verses before this, Christ once again gave the ability for all the disciples to recognize Him a third time through the breaking of the bread and sharing a meal as they did at the Last Supper celebrating the institution of the Eucharist. Some have argued if Jesus asked, "Peter do you love me?" Three times to remind him of his denial before the cock crowed as Christ was led to Calvary. If so, it would still be proof Jesus loves Peter unconditionally because despite his inability to acknowledge Christ during the greatest trial of his life, Jesus continues to place all of His trust in him to carry on the mission of the church.

Other scholars turn to the Greek for literal interpretation of what Jesus was really asking. The first two times Jesus says "Peter do you love me?" He uses the Greek word "agape" (ä-gä'pā) as the highest form of "all-encompassing" love. Peter's response is "Yes Lord, I love you." However, Peter's response is given with a different word for love, "phileo" (fill'-

E-o). This level of love would be normally used to say I love you like a "brother" or "friend." At this point, you would think Jesus might shake His head and dismiss Peter as to say, "He just can't love me the way I want him to." Instead, Jesus comes to meet Peter where he is in his life at that moment in the hopes over time he will reflect and grow into an all-encompassing love that Christ needs him to have. He does this by then saying to Peter in His final question, "Do you 'phileo' me?" Jesus worked the conversation from challenging Peter almost to a point of frustration to show how deeply He loves His disciple, but also, how deeply He desires Peter to love Him back. It wasn't a matter of worth; it was a matter of love. Just like with Peter, He sees you and I for what we are capable of and not merely the sins which have held us back.

As we come before the Lord during Mass to receive Him, we experience this type of unconditional love in the Eucharist. We receive a loving acceptance for where we are in our lives with the hope to pull us into a deeper level of adoration for what Christ offers us. He never looks to push us aside when our humanness makes us feel less than worthy or we've not fully realized the capability we have to be loved by Him. Praying for Him to come under our roof, healing our souls, is an open solicitation for the Lord to work wonders in our life. A chance to overcome any shortcoming we identify which separates us from His love. Like Dismas and the Centurion, it proves to the Lord, and ourselves, we are choosing Him over worldliness. It's almost as if Christ could be saying, "If you think I am worthy enough to be your 'all in all' to consume and heal you, then I believe you are worthy enough to receive me despite the falls you've had when your cross has been heavy."

Don't miss an opportunity to find and receive his "agape" love in the Eucharist because you wanted to be your own judge. Allow your invitation for Him to come under your roof to lead you to the table that always has a place for you to dine with the only One who accepts you the way you are. In that case, we can never be unworthy unless we are simply unwilling.

# SHARING THE JOURNEY:

*"I am Peter"*

*So often I have compared myself to Judas the betrayer. The one who sells you out when I am at my weakest. The one who breaks your heart when I fail to acknowledge all you do for me. However, tonight was different at Mass. Tonight I realized I am Peter. I beg to hear you say that I am the beloved. I want to be the one who is most revered; I forget the trust you place in me. Lord, I do not fully sell you out. I simply deny you even though I say I never would. I disregard the responsibility you place on me to be your voice in our church; the ways you build your word on my shoulders for the world to hear. Continually, you turn to me to give people your message as only I can; and they receive it. So many times people cannot hear what you are speaking directly to them and I am called to give them the right answer. I am Peter and I beg you to not lose hope in me and you continue to call me to build your church just as you did with your apostle Peter. Forgive me Lord when the cock has crowed or I may not have loved you as you desired but still you met me where I was. I know that I am Peter and that is a beautiful honor to be.*

# PRAYER:

*Dear Lord, help me to be reminded that I am worthy of your love. Grant me peace in my heart to not desire worldly affection or earthly praise as the way to measure how you see me. In the times I am afraid for my faith to shine through, give me courage to once again focus on the gift of you.*

# REFLECTION

_____

_____

_____

_____

_____

_____

_____

_____

_____

_____

_____

_____

_____

_____

_____

# III

# CONSUBSTANTIAL
## FOREVER BONDED AS ONE

---

*"As two pieces of wax fused together make one, so he who receives Holy Communion is so united with Christ that Christ is in him and he is in Christ." - St. Cyril of Alexandria*

---

**con·sub·stan·tial** [kän-səb-ˈstan(t)-shəl] - *adjective*
*Of the same kind or nature; having the same substance or essence; coessential*

Most of the time, I am not a fan of change. Although, when change happens in the church, there are many others right along with me; most of the time because it's something we don't understand or things take us out of our comfort zone.

There is one word which made its way into the Nicene Creed

which threatened to push me over the edge of "holy grumbling" into the stratosphere of flat out religious defiance: "Consubstantial." It replaced the phrase "One in being with the Father;" that phrase alone took me thirty years to figure out what it meant. It upset me so much, everywhere I went, I felt it was my cause to talk about how crazy it was they put this word into our creed. Worse yet, we replaced a phrase people didn't get the meaning of, to a word no one had ever heard of before. My arguments often resounded with a poignant phrase like "Yep that will help people pray deeper by making them say things they don't understand." With great humility I have to emphatically say, "Wow, was I wrong!"

Part of the beauty of our faith is to grow unconditionally by learning why we say the things we do. Understanding how poetic specific phrases, or words in this case, can be in their call to holiness for each of us. Realizing how truly inadequate our language is to describe accurately God's love, power, grace or union with us.

The moment which turned me around on the word "Consubstantial" was when a priest friend of mine finally stopped me in my tracks and explained its meaning. The image he used to peak my interest was the physical act of pouring one pitcher of water into another pitcher of water. Once this has been done, it literally becomes impossible to separate them. They are of the "same substance" leaving us unable to decipher which water was from which pitcher now that they are one. They existed separately, yet they are the same.

What the bishops are trying to tell us through the implementation of this particular word into the creed is that the Son is consubstantial with the Father. The entire Trinity exists as one single being despite being three separate Persons.

> The Church uses (I) the term "substance" (rendered also at times by "essence" or "nature") to designate the divine being in its unity, (II) the term "person" or "hypostasis" to designate the Father, Son and Holy Spirit in the real distinction among them, and (III) the term "relation" to designate the fact that their distinction lies in the relationship of each to the others.
>
> The Trinity is One. We do not confess three Gods, but one God in three persons, the "consubstantial Trinity". The divine persons do not share the one divinity among themselves but each of them is God whole and entire: "The Father is that which the Son is, the Son that which the Father is, the Father and the Son that which the Holy Spirit is, i.e. by nature one God." In the words of the Fourth Lateran Council (1215), "Each of the persons is that supreme reality, viz., the divine substance, essence or nature."
> (CCC 252-253)

For me, understanding how specific the word choice was, illustrated why I love the Tradition of the Church. It can take us from entry level participation to building a concrete foundation of teaching which helps us to understand some of the depth of God's amazing plan. A single word, "consubstantial," changed my heart from hating change to embracing the language so much I had to tell everyone why they should love it as well. Consubstantial now defines the very relationship I personally long for with Christ. A bond where nothing can tear us apart, nor any evil separate us. A connection found in the Eucharist.

When discussing our relationship with Christ we have to see

that the entire Trinity (Father, Son and Holy Spirit) becomes part of us as we receive the Eucharist. We become the church, we become the living tabernacle and we become the image of Christ for the world. Our hearts are no longer our own. Our encounter grows into a journey toward a consubstantial relationship.

Experiencing an eternal bond to God at that moment in the Eucharist calls us to look beyond our wants and instead seek to live a life where faith becomes part of everything we do. This doesn't happen out of guilt or obligation, it happens out of desire. If we seek a relationship with God, in the same manner that the Holy Trinity exists, then we are proclaiming we don't want to allow anything to come between us and our Lord. Faith can longer be a "take it or leave it" kind of proposition or even a part-time "check in and check out" mentality; it grows into a responsibility of love in relationship with Jesus Christ. You can't live without feeling Him at your side because He is not just part of the Church, but instead He is forever part of you. "If it is "daily bread," why do you take it once a year? Take daily what is to profit you daily. Live in such a way that you may deserve to receive it daily. He who does not deserve to receive it daily, does not deserve to receive it once a year." St. Ambrose of Milan

As a believer, we represent Jesus, and the Church, by identifying ourselves as Catholic Christians. Everything we do is a reflection of what we believe through our connection to God. We must be constantly aware that God in no way, shape or form is just placed on a shelf once we leave Mass, but instead is connected to all we are. Why is this so important to understand? We are the living tabernacle of our Lord who we have found through the Eucharist and that makes us accountable to the One we long to be consubstantial with every moment of our lives. Not only does it change how we go about our days, it also gives us endless opportunities to convert those who are lost and hopeless without the unconditional love of Christ.

If I said your name is only to be affiliated with you when you wanted to do good things and any other time you wanted to do bad stuff you could use an alias, eventually people would catch on. Their thoughts would become an association with the name you gave them at that moment. Full well knowing at any point you could switch up who you want to be. Trust would cease to exist because you weren't committed to being a quality individual who holds themselves to a higher standard all the time. How do you think Catholic Christians receive a negative image or any religious life for that matter? We have to move beyond part time church goer to become a committed Christian seeking a consubstantial relationship through the Eucharist. Everything becomes a trickle-down effect when we don't submit to this level of connection with the Savior. Trust me, I get it because I used to be that guy.

Consubstantial is a call to be one. Not only for our own personal relationship with Christ, but as a community of believers. It's how we all keep each other accountable. At the Last Supper, Christ gathered His apostles who would be the continuation of His church. When instituting the Eucharist that night He said a very direct phrase which gives us our directives and what it means to be community celebrating His feast: *"Do this in memory of me."* (Luke 22:19) Everything we are, say and do is in His memory. It wasn't a request for certain disciples to think about Jesus at certain parts of the feast, while partially commit to the ministry Jesus called them into.

> *"Since all the faithful form one body, the good of each is communicated to the others...We must therefore believe that there exists a communion of goods in the Church. But the most important member is Christ, since he is the head...Therefore, the riches of Christ are communicated to all the members, through the sacraments. As this Church is governed by one and the same Spirit, all the goods she has received necessarily become a common fund." (CCC 947)*

He wants all of us to dine in the manner to unconditionally accept Him as our identity.

If we are one family, we become responsible in new ways to represent the Kingdom here on Earth by staying connected to our call. By finding Jesus in the Eucharist, we also find every person who is part of the communion of saints in Heaven who offered themselves to be a vessel of His love. We are that one community who is forever bound together through the death and resurrection of our Lord given to us time and time again when He presents Himself in the Blessed Sacrament of the Altar. Not only are you dining with those present in the church, you are sharing the Bread of Life with every person you love who has gone before you. Every Saint who gave their life for what they found to be truth. Any person who ever inspired you to want to be more in this life or shared their time with you to help you grow in faith. We would give anything to have one more chance to share a meal with the loved ones who have passed on to eternal life. Although that's not possible, what a delight it is to know they are part of us each time we feast on the Eucharist. A consubstantial communion of saints, embracing Heaven together at one moment, sharing in the same Lord.

If I had to summarize the beauty of working toward a con-substantial relationship with the entire Trinity through the Eucharist it would be this: The only way we can move into a deeper, more connected level of faith is through commit-ment. A commitment which doesn't allow the things of this world to separate us from The Father, The Son or The Holy Spirit. It is only through our conviction and realization of how blessed we are to be connected to Christ through the Eucharist that we will be able to feel a connection which calls us to unconditionally look for any way we can experience a closeness to Him. Our mass then simply isn't something we do; it becomes who we are.

# SHARING THE JOURNEY:

*To know you is to love you, to see you is to feel you, to be one with you is to touch the edge of Heaven. Enter me Lord as your vessel, your light, your hope, to shine and bring your Kingdom close enough for others to experience.*

*Sheer beauty surrounds me, each breathe I take is one of unity with Him. Timeless moments are but only a glimpse into the power of His love. I sit in AWE with a sense of wonder... how much I am loved and how extremely calming only the PEACE He can provide is... Thank you Jesus for you have humbled me in your presence again.*

# PRAYER:

*Lord, you are with me everywhere and always. I pray that I can decrease so all the amazing gifts you offer me through the eucharist allow others to see i am forevever connected to you. to be one with you now and forever is where I hope to always be.*

# Reflection

_____

_____

_____

_____

_____

_____

_____

_____

_____

_____

_____

_____

_____

_____

_____

_____

# IV

# MARY MOST HOLY
## RECEIVING THE BLESSED MOTHER

---

*"Never be afraid of loving the Blessed
Virgin too much. You can never love her
more than Jesus did."*
~St. Maximilian Colbe

---

Mary is always one of the main focuses for those who want to debate or criticize certain traditions in our Catholic faith. People have challenged me on the Catholic "worship" of Mary perceived by other denominations of Christianity. Just a quick reminder to all: We do not "worship" Mary. We hold her in the highest regard as the mother of Christ chosen by God as the one worthy enough to carry, birth and raise His Son. So, you still might be asking yourself, "Isn't this a book on the Eucharist? And the Eucharist is the presence of Christ, not Mary." In this case, you would be correct and so very wrong at the same time.

I once emceed an ecumenical event for various Christian denominations. After an evening which was filled with great music and an opportunity for me to evangelize about the beauty of a life centered on Jesus Christ, a few attendees became aware that I was Catholic. These people immediately wanted to dig deeper into the theological aspects of Catholicism, primarily the manner that we have placed Mary above Christ. Politely, I listened to the challenge they placed before me and waited for my turn to respond. While explaining we do not place Mary above Christ, nor do we actually pray "to" her but rather "through" her: I wanted to ask two of the women a question back. "How is it, that as a woman who is a believer in Jesus Christ, you don't seek the intercession of Mary? After all, isn't it her example of obedience to God's will what you desire in your own life?" Very puzzled they continued to stare at me while I followed up with, "As a matter of fact, to remain a faith filled disciples, shouldn't you actually long to identify with her more closely to love her Son more deeply?" I wasn't trying to prove any single point or belittle their misunderstanding of the role Mary holds in our church, I wanted them to understand that if we believe the scriptures by which we define truth, we cannot discount the length God went to choose one woman over all to be worthy enough to carry His son.

> "We believe that the Holy Mother of God, the new Eve, Mother of the Church, continues in heaven to exercise her maternal role on behalf of the members of Christ" (Paul VI, CPG § 15). (CCC 975)

Mary is not a female to be discounted or simply a peace of flesh Jesus needed to have a traditional birth. The Catechism again states:

> Mary's role in the Church is inseparable from her union with Christ and flows directly from it. "This union of the mother with the Son in the work of salvation is made

*manifest from the time of Christ's virginal conception up
to his death"; it is made manifest above all at the hour of
his Passion:*

*Thus the Blessed Virgin advanced in her pilgrimage of
faith, and faithfully persevered in her union with her Son
unto the cross. There she stood, in keeping with the divine plan, enduring with her only begotten Son the inten-
sity of his suffering, joining herself with his sacrifice in her
mother's heart, and lovingly consenting to the immola-
tion of this victim, born of her: to be given, by the same
Christ Jesus dying on the cross, as a mother to his disciple, with these words: "Woman, behold your son."
(CCC 964)*

She was part of all of it. The woman given by God, from the
cross, to be our mother; Mary most holy, mother of all. So
in receiving Jesus Christ into our lives and certainly into our
souls through the Eucharist, the beauty of Mary is part of it
all.

To understand Mary's role in the Eucharist, we have to first
examine her courage to say "yes" to God's will over her own
desires. However, we cannot do this without going back to
the original Hebrew scriptures which describe the items that
represented previous covenants God made with His people.
This Old Testament knowledge gives us insight of how
highly regarded God expects us to see Mary.

The Ark of the Covenant in the Old Testament held three
things: Manna from Heaven, their daily bread, The Staff of
Aaron, the High Priest after Moses and The Ten Command-
ment Tablets, the law. (Heb 9:4) These items were hidden
within the golden Ark as it was carried from land to land; it
was the most beloved treasure of the Jewish people. Never
touched with human hands and with a tent placed over it

whenever they rested.

In our Catholic Christian faith, we identify Christ as the "New Covenant" through the Eucharist. Christ is the New and everlasting Covenant bringing people to the promised land of Heaven. Jesus embodied the complete contents of the items carried in the original Ark of the Covenant: His Body as the new Manna (Bread of Life), He is the true high priest (originally represented by the Staff of Aaron) and He is the living word of the new law which was once written as the Ten Commandments on stone tablets. Since Mary held Jesus within her womb when He already possessed what He needed bring salvation to this world, we refer to Mary as, "The Ark of the New Covenant."

This is why the first reading at the vigil mass for The Feast of the Assumption is from the book of Chronicles which describes King David having the Ark brought to the place which he prepared for it. On the actual day of the Assumption our readings come from Revelations which foretell us of the Ark in the heavens being opened and a woman *"Clothed with the moon under her feet and on her head a crown of twelve stars. She was with child and wailed aloud in pain as she labored to give birth."* (Rev. 12:1-2)

The fact that Mary was willing to become the "Ark of the New Covenant," as the vessel, which would hold Christ unconditionally within her womb. God incarnate lay within her, sleeping and awaiting His birth. This revelation is directly tied to our willingness to take Christ into ourselves and become His living tabernacle. If we do not take on the nurturing nature of the same Christ who lives within us, then we are not answering the same call.

> *"Mary, in whom the Lord himself has just made his dwelling, is the daughter of Zion in person, the ark of the covenant, the place where the glory of the Lord dwells. She is "the dwelling of God... with men." (CCC 2676)*

We must rely on her to be our guide and at the same time our intercessory to gain access to all we become when we find Jesus in the Eucharist.

As the first tabernacle we see Christ's presence already recognizable to the faithful even while He lay in Mary's womb. Just as Elizabeth experienced upon Mary's arrival:

> *"When Elizabeth heard Mary's greeting, the infant leaped in her womb, and Elizabeth, filled with the holy Spirit, cried out in a loud voice and said, "Most blessed are you among women, and blessed is the fruit of your womb. And how does this happen to me, that the mother of my Lord should come to me? For at the moment the sound of your greeting reached my ears, the infant in my womb leaped for joy.* (Lk 1:41-44)

She knew the baby Mary was carrying was her Lord even before Mary could tell her. John the Baptist "leaped" inside of Elizabeth once she approached allowing us to realize the connection not only they would instantly have, but for us to realize all life is bound by the One who is our Messiah.

As the Christ child grew and the journey continued on to Bethlehem, Joseph also felt the real presence of Christ within the womb even when He could not see what he believed. St. Peter Julien Eymard said it best as he explains the correlation between Elizabeth and John's moment relating it to how Joseph must have felt laying next to the Messiah every night even before He was born; it becomes a model of the same adoration we continue to celebrate in the Eucharist:

> *"Words cannot express the perfection of his adoration. If Saint John leaped in the womb at the approach of Mary, what feelings must have coursed through Joseph during those six months when he had at his side and under his very eyes the hidden God! If the father of Origen used to kiss his child during the night and adore the Holy Spirit living within Him, can we doubt that Joseph must often have adored Jesus hidden in the pure tabernacle of Mary? How fervent that adoration must have been: My Lord and my God, behold your servant! No one can describe the adoration of this noble soul. He saw nothing, yet he believed; his faith had to pierce the virginal veil of Mary. So likewise with you! Under the veil of the Sacred Species your faith must see our Lord. Ask St. Joseph for his Lively, constant faith."*

Her entire life was always going to be about her role as Jesus' mother. From the manner in which her relationship with Joseph would be lived out until the time she nudged Jesus to perform His first miracle at the Wedding Feast of Cana. Mary never became anything less than the woman chosen by God to not only be His son's mother, but to be our mother. The woman who represented the New Covenant carried not only the word of God made flesh, but the One who became the bread of life. We must see her as more than just a woman who birthed Christ.

Even in our churches, Mary's importance goes beyond simple holy days of obligation or May crowning ceremonies. With the new creation she helped bring into the world in order to restore it, she is the new Eve; Christ is the new Adam. Together, the story of salvation springs forth to take the one born without sin to nurture the One who would take away the sins of the world.

Even with understanding her role and remaining obedient to God, we can still identify with her humanness when things didn't go as she expected. In Mary's "yes" to give birth to Christ, she never could have imagined it would also mean she would have to watch her baby she raised to a man be savagely beaten and die a slow death hanging from the cross He was nailed to. How heart-broken Mary must have been watching her son breathe His last breath. Actually it is described that her soul left her body conjoined with the Son of Man at the time of His death. Each of the sorrows Mary had to experience must have caused unexplainable grief. There is a connection to the grace in which she was able to handle all of her responsibility unconditionally despite the grief which came along with it.

So as we approach the Eucharist, there is a part of us connected to that moment at the cross when Jesus looks down upon her one last time. *"When Jesus saw his mother - and the disciple there whom he loved, he said to his mother, 'Woman, behold, your son.' Then he said to the disciple, 'Behold, your mother.' And from that hour the disciple took her into his home."* (John 19: 26-27) It is His sacrifice as He waits in those final moments which sends Him on the journey to His Heavenly Father only to give us the gift of Mary to share in as well.

Mary held Christ in her womb. He fed off her, her blood would have sustained His life until the time His blood sustained ours. Additionally, if Mary the Mother of Christ (God incarnate) allowed the infant Jesus to suckle her breast in order to be fed for life to remain in Him, then are we not connected by same nourishment in which we feed on through Jesus Christ? Mother Therese tells us, "The 'yes' of Mary gave us the Holy Eucharist, as the body of Jesus was formed from the Immaculate Heart of His Mother, from whose flesh Jesus took the flesh He gives us in the Blessed Sacrament." God chose Mary to nurse Jesus in every way possible, both literally and figuratively. Her connection to Christ is no different than any mother to a son and so to us.

Finally, let's view it from this perspective. Any mother can understand a love for their child and willingness to look down at that babe in their arms desiring a glorious future for them. A destiny of dreams fulfilled and happiness at every possible moment. Then one day her young man is offered up for the crowds not for what He has done wrong but what He has given the world; a world blinded by ignorance. For us to receive Mary's love in the sacrificed Christ is a testament to her faithfulness to remain at His side until the end of time. So too, we shall remain next to Him always in the Eucharist.

After we have received Christ, we house the living Savior to share with the world. To nurture His image through all we do. It is within our inner being that He continues to draw life and remain the risen Christ. If for no other reason, we share the bond with Mary to be both maternal and paternal in order for the Lord to enter the world through us. Mary gave birth to the Lamb on which we are fed, nourished and redeemed. Now, we are the ones to sustain the life of Christ through our own Fiat ("Let it be done") and Amen when we acknowledge we believe by receiving the Lord. A similar yes to what Mary willingly and unselfishly offered of herself before the Angel without condition.

# SHARING THE JOURNEY:

*When struggling with a decision that you say yes to for the Lord, think back on Mary and the pain that her "yes" caused her to watch her son die. But I guarantee if you asked her if she would changer her answers she would not because her decision was of God and brought the ultimate healer into this world. A yes does not always mean "easy."*

*Jesus I know you are capable of comforting me through your love and tenderness. But there is nothing more comforting than the arms of a Mother when we seek peace. I pray that your Mother Mary surrounds us with love to give me the comfort I long for in moments of fear. I also pray for my wife and daughter to serve you as she did so they will be glorified one day in Heaven by living through her example.*

# PRAYER:

*Mother Mary, it was your obedience which allowed you to be the living vessel for Christ to enter the world. As we receive the Eucharist we acknowledge your presence in your role of who Christ was able to become through all the ways you nurtured Him. We pray for your intercession as we ask you to lift us up to your Son, Jesus Christ, so we may continue to honor you by all the ways we continually bring Him into the world each day.*

# REFLECTION

_____

_____

_____

_____

_____

_____

_____

_____

_____

_____

_____

_____

_____

_____

# V

# TEMPTATION IN THE DESERT
## OVERCOMING SPIRITUAL BATTLES

---

*"Even though the Lord is in us, He still wants us to ask for what we desire."*
*~St. Padre Pio*

---

One of the most difficult aspects of surrendering to a life in Christ is accepting we will be tempted over and over again by the Evil one who longs to steal our mind, heart and soul from the Father. Spiritual warfare is real, but not something we talk about enough as we strive to live a virtuous life. In the Eucharist we find Christ remaining steadfast during His own temptations. I want to explore a little more deeply the unconditional trust Christ had when he encountered the devil while fasting in the desert. Throughout our journey we will need to call on the same level of trust in our Father when we are left alone with our thoughts and a tempter who seeks to see us fall away from any and all belief in our faith; especially being the person God has called us to be for ourselves, our family and others in the world we encounter who need a relationship with our Lord.

It's true, when we begin to talk about the devil, people immediately dismiss the "crazy talk" with a pre conceived, horror film interpretation of the horned creature we call Satan. Before my own conversion, if anyone would have told me certain strife and sin came into my life through the work of the devil, I would have immediately shunned any effort they placed forth to help me grow in my faith. However, our foe is much more cunning, persuasive and normal looking than we could ever imagine. There are people who walk away from their faith after a major conversion because they are unaware how to handle the spiritual battle waged on them after they turn their life over to God. Until we actually acknowledge who, or what we are fighting against, we cannot fully understand how to combat the temptation to sin which comes our way.

We often find ourselves frustrated by what would seem to be a cruel joke. We lovingly except Christ into our heart through the Eucharist and God rewards us by allowing us to succumb to the arrows the devil shoots at us. It's in these times we must gaze upon Christ in the Sacrament and know he endured the same trials. Jesus went from immediately being baptized (Mt. 3:13-17) to forty days fasting in the desert. (Mt. 4:1-11) This is the same thing we are asked to do when we reach a new level of spirituality. Bathed in the Spirit we are released to the world that tries to offer us more than they think God can. We must shut out the precepts of the world and the distractions around us to fully absorb what we might be called into once we have been opened up in new ways. For Christ, it was a time to prepare Himself to lead the disciples be able to carry on the church after He returned to the Father. For you and I, it's the same. Our call is to be His church and share his evangelization day in and day out in the real world.

> Jesus' temptation reveals the way in which the Son of God is Messiah, contrary to the way Satan proposes to him and the way men wish to attribute to him. This is why Christ vanquished the Tempter for us: "For we have not a high priest who is unable to sympathize with our weaknesses, but one who in every respect has been tested as we are, yet without sinning." By the solemn forty days of Lent the Church unites herself each year to the mystery of Jesus in the desert. (CCC 540)

One of my favorite artistic interpretations of Jesus' temptation in the desert is found through the simplicity of a still image cartoon entitled "40" by British Illustrator, Si Smith. In this illustration, at the point in which the devil appears to tempt Christ, Smith has taken the liberty to depict Satan as a mirror image of Christ himself. While the entire cartoon is done in black and white, only the reflection image of "Satan" is shaded and outlined in red. While the black and white image of Jesus at this point is withdrawn, tired and weary, the colored image of the devil is without blemish, energetic and wide eyed. The suggestion the artist makes is that temptation often times comes from within. While we are off looking for blatant injustices and evils, the devil is working from within to get us to make decisions against what we believe. It is quite the image to prove we can be our own worst enemies. Satan will do anything he can to get us to seek ways to please ourselves rather than our Father in Heaven.

We can place lots of blame on ourselves for the times we succumb to sinning and do not discern within ourselves the cause of the sin in the first place. Overcome with guilt, we do not look to identify the root of our evils. The littlest of sins can make us so weak we are unable to ward off the advances of the evil one. This is why we pray in the *Our Father*, "*Lead us not into temptation but deliver us from evil.*" (Mt.6:12)

> "This petition goes to the root of the preceding one, for our sins result from our consenting to temptation; we therefore ask our Father not to "lead" us into temptation. It is difficult to translate the Greek verb used by a single English word: the Greek means both "do not allow us to enter into temptation" and "do not let us yield to temptation." "God cannot be tempted by evil and he himself tempts no one"; on the contrary, he wants to set us free from evil. We ask him not to allow us to take the way that leads to sin. We are engaged in the battle "between flesh and spirit"; this petition implores the Spirit of discernment and strength." (CCC 2846)

I heard a presenter once talk about how good the devil is at getting us to work against our own selves. He explained it by saying that the devil reminds us of the "merciful" God we have in order to get our guard down for us to commit sin. A whisper of "Go ahead and do it, God will forgive you in the end because He has to." Immediately, once we have committed the offense, he then loudly belittles us with a reminder of what a "just" God we have, working to convince us there is no hope; God could not love a sinner like us. The devil calls us to remember the "Old Testament God" who offered wrath and sickness to those who veered off course. We begin to look at our self and hate the very person we are, not because we don't desire grace, but we fear the actions of any one moment that causes us to be shunned from the love of God; thrown into the fires of hell. Instead, what we really have is the same person of God in the Trinity, in Jesus Christ, who hung on the cross extending to mercy proclaiming, *"Forgive them Father for they know not what they do."* (Lk 23:34) He knew what temptation was like in the desert, in the Garden and every other place in between where the devil worked to thwart His purpose. He knows mercy must be continually offered to us until we spend eternity in Heaven. The Eucharist fills us to be showered with the blood of the Lamb who spoke whose words.

As I stated before, the notion of spiritual warfare or mere talk of the devil as a real thing would have sent me to dismiss any person who believed deeply in this fairy tale image I created of Satan in my own world. However, it wasn't until I was able to begin to identify all the ways I would let him get to me that I actually understand what to pray for. We must be aware of his presence in order to stop his efforts before they begin to derail us. The devil is smart and it's why he uses temptation to persuade you, rather than just forcing you to do sinful acts or have fearful thoughts through intimidation. After all, he is the prince of darkness who stopped at nothing while he revolted against God and his fellow angels. I am sure his might could scare us all into submission if we allowed him. One thing he fears though is the name of "Jesus." We can then take it one step further that if he fears merely his name, how strong can we be against him if we receive and take on the body, blood, soul and divinity of our Savior? That he can never touch.

In the Eucharist we find the foundation of the word which

Christ used to fight off the temptations of Satan in the desert, and it also becomes clear the manner in which we need to fall back on what we believe to not only identify the devil's attempts, but to drive him away from any moment he is meddling in our lives. While we receive the knowledge to know temptation exists, it means nothing without knowing we also receive the courage to overcome it in the Eucharist. When we gaze upon the Eucharist we have to look as if our heart is begging, "Lord, you know my struggles to remain faithful to your word, allow me to remain courageous in your image."

Lastly, beware of one of the most effective temptations that wins out more than any other: apathy. Not a blatant action to hurt or disobey God, but a redirection of thoughts away from all the things which can fulfill you through faith. It's a level of indifference which causes inaction to be a distraction toward anything else other than being who, where or what God wants you to be. The "Confeitor" prayer we offer at Mass gives us the line "In what I have done and *what I have failed to do.*" We examine our conscience and look for ways we have acted out against God or specific sins we committed so we may seek forgiveness. In the same light, we seek forgiveness for our lack of action when we choose to look the other way rather than serve His Kingdom.

How often are we searching for the times we made to pray and chose to browse the Internet instead? When did we have an opportunity to be the hands and feet of Christ for another but turned a blind eye to their needs for self-serving desires of our own? This temptation can often be the easiest to succumb to and the hardest to recognize because we talk ourselves into it. We can certainly justify why something else takes precedence over discipleship. We create a reality in our mind fed by the devil which points to a life we are entitled to have.

The devil is trying to place fear and anger in our heart when his advances offer us "better" things than what God gives us. In these moments it is spiritual warfare which has been launched to dissuade you from relying on God to help turn things around for us. We find ourselves looking for Earthly possessions and self-serving pleasure to fix things our self; all the while, the devil smiles. Within the battle he is offering us things our weakness cannot refute. There are the things that put Mass, church events and faith opportunities on hold because of "something" better. Just like Christ we must return to God by leaning on what got us to this point of our faith journey.

> The Holy Spirit makes us discern between trials, which are necessary for the growth of the inner man, and temptation, which leads to sin and death. We must also discern between being tempted and consenting to temptation. Finally, discernment unmasks the lie of temptation, whose object appears to be good, a "delight to the eyes" and desirable, when in reality its fruit is death.
> (CCC 2847)

Finding Jesus' strength and courage in the Eucharist is vital to overcome temptation. We focus once again on Christ and allow the word made flesh to do battle with the evil one. All the struggles as well as the grace Jesus possessed are present in the Eucharist. "He humbled Himself to share in our humanity so we might come to share in His divinity." So too is His ability to see the Father's will win out over the cunning efforts of the devil. By receiving the Host containing Christ we are filled with what it takes to be obedient, to remain faithful so joy becomes our goal instead of pleasure, while the Happiness we seek is of Heaven and not the temporary home on Earth. Pray when you consume Him to let nothing be more important than your faithfulness to the father and that truth wins out over human desires.

# SHARING THE JOURNEY:

*My time with you Lord is never enough and when we share time it reminds me of how much it sustains me. Protect me from my trials and the urges that Satan may place in front of me, my family and those I love.*

*"Be still my child and you will know all I have planned for you. Take time to be one with me and let the sound of my voice nourish your thoughts and place peace in your heart. You are mine and that is always enough regardless of ALL you face."*

# PRAYER:

*Heavenly Father, send your angels to surround me and give me the strength to ward off all attempts by the evil one who works to lead me away from you. In Jesus' image may I be glorified by your Word to know truth despite Satan's empty promises.*

# REFLECTION

# VI

# A PARALYTIC, AN ADULTERESS & THE BETRAYER
## HEALING, FORGIVENESS & REDEMPTION

---

*"The Eucharist bathes the tormented soul in light and love. Then the soul appreciates these words, 'Come all you who are sick, I will restore your health.'"*
*~ St. Bernadette Soubirous*

---

One of the most beautiful attributes we will ever find through Jesus in the Eucharist is His willingness to unconditionally forgive us. His desire to extend us mercy when we acknowledge our need for it and look to right our wrongs.

Before we go too deep, we have to remember that our hearts and souls must be prepared in order to receive Christ, however by bringing Him physically into us there is an unbelievable opportunity to reconnect with God despite any separation we have experienced do to sin. We'll talk more about Reconciliation later, for now I want to invite you to focus on the incredible gift we are offered through our Savior in the grace of His mercy. As we come before the Eucharist and take Christ into us we are made whole of our venial (less offensive) sins:

> *"As bodily nourishment restores lost strength, so the Eucharist strengthens our charity, which tends to be weakened in daily life; and this living charity wipes away venial sins" (CCC 1394)*

Forgiveness is a critical part of all our lives. It can be the difference maker which determines a path we continue down in a friendship, whether or not a marriage withstands the strains placed on it over time and quite possibly dictate if a family is able to spend the holidays together. No matter the situation, one thing is for certain: a lack of forgiveness is toxic. Jesus knows this and as He presents Himself over and over to us in the Eucharist, each time He instills in us our ability to forgive as if He is repeating the same words he offered in the Gospel of Matthew:

> *Come to me, all you who labor and are burdened, and I will give you rest. Take my yoke upon you and learn from me, for I am meek and humble of heart; and you will find rest for yourselves. For my yoke is easy, and my burden light. (Mt 11:28-30)*

Directly relating to the Eucharist itself, we can feel the prophetic statement made at the Last Supper of His purpose on this Earth, *"this is my blood of the covenant, which will be shed on behalf of many for the forgiveness of sins."* (Mt

26:28) Expounded upon even further in our Catholic teaching:

> "Holy Communion separates us from sin. The body of Christ we receive in Holy Communion is "given up for us," and the blood we drink "shed for the many for the forgiveness of sins." For this reason the Eucharist cannot unite us to Christ without at the same time cleansing us from past sins and preserving us from future sins."
> (CCC 1392)

If we are willing to accept the redemption of Christ on the cross, then we must be consumed with that same salvation found in His real presence of the Eucharist. A salvation granted to each of us and shared with the people we encounter unconditionally. Mercy is key not just for the world to feel loved, but for what we harbor inside which we tend to think can make us unlovable.

Why is forgiveness so important? It seems like a straightforward answer, however the power of forgiveness is able to heal both parties involved; the wounded and even more importantly the wounder. As C.S. Lewis puts it "Forgiving and being forgiven are two names for the same thing. The important thing is that a discord has been resolved."

So let's relate this to the physical act of consuming forgiveness through the Eucharist. Jesus was a healer that much we know. Countless miracles were performed and the lame were made anew by the power of His touch. All of these acts were done without condition of the person's past, their motives for coming to the Lord and certainly offered unconditionally to not only cure physical ailments but to restore emotional ailments as well. The stories of Christ's willingness to make people whole are countless, but they all culminate with the forgiveness of sins. Throughout scripture we witness this in various manners.

To best highlight this, I want to concentrate three different acts of forgiveness offered by Christ in the Gospels that highlight not only His desire to make people whole, but also the role other people play in these special healings. Christ seemingly was able to forgive the unforgivable. As we study these three different accounts, take note how they vary in needs and occurred without judgement.

## A PARALYTIC (MARK 2:1-5)

*When Jesus returned to Capernaum after some days, it became known that he was at home. Many gathered together so that there was no longer room for them, not even around the door, and he preached the word to them. They came bringing to him a paralytic carried by four men. Unable to get near Jesus because of the crowd, they opened up the roof above him. After they had broken through, they let down the mat on which the paralytic was lying. When Jesus saw their faith, he said to the paralytic, "Child, your sins are forgiven."*

What I love about this aspect of forgiveness told through the "Healing of the Paralytic" is the role others played in getting their friend to the only One who would be able to heal him.

The first thing we need to admire is the resilience of the man's friends. They only planned to take their friend to Jesus, however they couldn't have anticipated the crowds, nor been prepared to break through the roof to get their friend to Him. Still, they did not give up. Instead they were persistent which becomes key to Jesus' healing of the man. We can only imagine how they would have had to claw, dig and scratch their way through brick, clay and mud in order get the roof open, all without possessing the proper tools necessary. A painful, tedious process putting their own well-being at risk filled with pain and unceasing determination.

Secondly, we really don't find out about the "heart" of the paralytic who is being lowered to Christ. Sure, his friends wanted to get him there, but we never here words spoken by the man of his own desire to be made whole. Maybe he is weak, frail and unable to speak. Possibly, he is bitter, sad or broken by the disability which most likely made him ostracized by others of the time. It never really tells us whether he had a choice in the matter or believed in what Jesus could do for him. Was he born that way or had he made a decision that resulted in the brokenness, which incapacitated him? In the end, none of these assumptions matter.

Jesus ultimately heals the man because of the faith by the ones who brought him. He takes note of the great love they have for their friend and their faith to know the only way he can walk again is through the power of Jesus. Christ forgives his sins, gives him the gift to be fully functioning; all because Jesus saw the faith of friends caring for another more man they cared about themselves. This man was brought to the Savoir by believers who knew Christ was the way, truth and life.

Each and every day we have the opportunity to lead others to Christ. The Eucharist offers us strength to take those who need His love and bring them to where they need to be in order to see Him. Sure they may not choose to accept it at first or even recognize Him when He is at work in front of their eyes. Still, we must be the friends who bring the broken to the One who can forgive and heal. Invite them to Mass. Share scripture with them. Enlighten their hearts on the beauty of the Eucharist which might just be the encounter they need to mend their brokenness at the feet of Jesus. No matter what, make the effort.

Certainly, there will be days we are paralyzed with fear or hurt and the greatest hope we can receive from others is that they will pick us up and lead us to Christ who will forgive whatever is necessary so we can be healed fully. Whether we are tattered or someone else is wounded, when we receive the Eucharist, we gain an awareness of mercy to open up during this precious opportunity. A chance to pray in thanksgiving for our relationship with Christ. A time to search our hearts for the people we know so desperately need to find Him in the Eucharist as well. If we can lead them to the Sacrament through our faith, a healing may take place to convert another heart to the Kingdom. We might even hear a whisper saying, "Child your sins are forgiven." (Mark 2:5)

## AN ADULTERESS (LK 8:3-11)

*Then the scribes and the Pharisees brought a woman who had been caught in adultery and made her stand in the middle. They said to him, "Teacher, this woman was caught in the very act of committing adultery. Now in the law, Moses commanded us to stone such women. So what do you say?" They said this to test him, so that they could have some charge to bring against him. Jesus bent down and began to write on the ground with his finger. But when they continued asking him, he straightened up and said to them, "Let the one among you who is without sin be the first to throw a stone at her." Again he bent down and wrote on the ground. And in response, they went away one by one, beginning with the elders. So he was left alone with the woman before him. Then Jesus straightened up and said to her, "Woman, where are they? Has no one condemned you?" She replied, "No one, sir." Then Jesus said, "Neither do I condemn you. Go, [and] from now on do not sin any more."*

This is a powerful witness of a sinner being condemned to death to the extent of the law by an angry mob. No leeway for mercy at all. Politically, it's another opportunity for the Pharisees to trap Jesus into deciding between Jewish law (immediate stoning) and Roman law (trial and sentencing by judge). However, by initially only using his finger to write in the sand and choosing to heal the soul of the women, Jesus instead turns this story into a beautiful moment of forgiveness without condemnation. He then calls out all those present with their venom and judgment by looking for the one without sin who could cast the first stone. Seemingly to condemn their harsh reaction to the situation even more so than the woman' sin.

Yes, Jesus knew she did wrong since she was caught in the act. Nonetheless, He immediately steps between her and the people who wanted to harm her. He protects her from the threat until it is gone so He can speak directly to her. How many times does He step between us and the danger of the foes we have in our midst?

Christ didn't want an explanation from the woman. He only sought to bring a lost child back to the Kingdom by not swiftly condemning her and instead offering reconciliation to encourage her to sin no more. This exchange can be placed in our ears, as the Real Presence is placed on our tongue during Communion. His calming and tender voice reaffirming our heart that our actions can always be reconciled and while the world may look to constantly denounce the sinner, He knows we are more than our sin and loves us unconditionally. He longs to end the separation our actions can place between us and Him. A distance immediately removed when we find His forgiveness in the Eucharist

The reconciliation of the unnamed adulteress that takes place has a trickle-down effect because of the way He handles the situation. Those who could not cast the first stone also would have soul searching to do. Yes, we focus on the woman's redemption, but we must not miss an opportunity to change all hearts when Christ is present. If we can deal with our own adversaries calmly toward resolution, not only do we diffuse the immediate threat, we may also redeem the unintended soul. Our redemption is revealed through our awareness that Christ was sacrificed by these same types of people. In the Eucharist we receive the glorified body of the resurrection which overshadows all immediate threats who look to oppress our personal opportunities for healing to take place.

> "Death is swallowed up in victory. Where, O death, is your victory? Where, O death, is your sting? The sting of death is sin, and the power of sin is the law. But thanks be to God who gives us the victory through our Lord Jesus Christ." (1 Cor 15:54-57)

So before we want to convict others or we are surrounded by those who wish to see us suffer for our mistakes, let us remember what St Paul said to the Ephesians:

*"All bitterness, fury, anger, shouting, and reviling must be removed from you, along with all malice. [And] be kind to one another, compassionate, forgiving one another as God has forgiven you in Christ." (Eph 4:31-32)*

# THE BETRAYER
# (MT 26:14-16, 20-25 & LK 22:47-48)

*Then one of the Twelve, who was called Judas Iscariot, went to the chief priests and said, "What are you willing to give me if I hand him over to you?" They paid him thirty pieces of silver, and from that time on he looked for an opportunity to hand him over. (Mt 26:14-16)*

*When it was evening, he reclined at table with the Twelve. And while they were eating, he said, "Amen, I say to you, one of you will betray me." Deeply distressed at this, they began to say to him one after another, "Surely it is not I, Lord?" He said in reply, "He who has dipped his hand into the dish with me is the one who will betray me. The Son of Man indeed goes, as it is written of him, but woe to that man by whom the Son of Man is betrayed. It would be better for that man if he had never been born." Then Judas, his betrayer, said in reply, "Surely it is not I, Rabbi?" He answered, "You have said so." (Mt 26:20-25)*

*While he was still speaking, a crowd approached and in front was one of the Twelve, a man named Judas. He went up to Jesus to kiss him. Jesus said to him, "Judas, are you betraying the Son of Man with a kiss?" (Lk 22:47-48)*

In the scripture above, I chose to combine the two different authors (Matthew and Luke) because there are many emotions stirred up when we hear this part of the Passion. How could Judas plan to offer Jesus up? If Jesus knew who would betray Him, why didn't He put an end to it? Why did Judas have to identify the Messiah with a kiss? Christ knew how things had to be in order to fulfill His Father's plan. Likewise, in our lives, there are people we meet, or even seasons of friends that involve others who betray us. There are people who are part of the challenge we face as we strive to be who we were created to be as a child of God. They bring about confrontations where blame and rage could rule the day before forgiveness ever enters our mind. Christ offers us the example we need to follow during these situations.

As a character, we see Judas as the person who killed Jesus with his betrayal. Not only did Judas' actions create sin for him, it also brought all of the soldiers who would now need to be forgiven for their role. Judas' action was simply the opening of a gateway for the entire journey to Calvary to take place. A spiral effect which included those who would hold the whips, spit in the face of Christ, deny Him by choosing a murderer to go free instead of Jesus, drive nail marks into His hands and mock Him till the final lance pierced His side. Judas' sin didn't only harm the two people involved, it shattered the very being of humanity while Jesus was led to death. The Baltimore Catechism tells us this about Judas:

> "Judas, one of His Apostles, betrayed Our Lord, and from His sin we may learn that even the good may become very wicked by the abuse of their free will." (Baltimore Catechism 380)

Still, despite the enormity of what Judas did and all it culminated into, it's still forgiven in the eyes of God.

In our unwillingness to forgive, we are not giving full attention to the causes which lead others to harm through words, actions and even inaction. A role the devil has a hand in to hurt the faithful and possibly lead them to forget Who they truly belong to. For Judas, was it really his actions that led him to betray his friend? A man he walked with, watched perform miracles and One who trusted Judas with the prized bag holding their treasury. We find powerful words in scripture both before the betrayal and right before Judas flees from The Last Supper; the accounts highlight the power of the evil one's role in sin.

> Before the betrayal: "Then Satan entered into Judas, the one surnamed Iscariot, who was counted among the Twelve" (Lk 22:3)

> At the last supper: "Jesus answered, "It is the one to whom I hand the morsel after I have dipped it." So he dipped the morsel and [took it and] handed it to Judas, son of Simon the Iscariot. After he took the morsel, Satan entered him. So Jesus said to him, 'What you are going to do, do quickly.'" (Jn 13:26-27)

I believe every one of us has the ability to be "Judas' kiss." We can all relate to Judas for the times we sell out Christ for other worldly possessions because evil assists in getting us to forget whom we should remain loyal to. Yet, Christ still looks at us with His tender loving eyes and knows our humanness has its darkest of moments we cannot erase. The same eyes that looked down on Judas as he realized what he done from the moment the soldiers seized His Lord.

Through receiving His compassionate stare in the Eucharist, it pierces the portions of our soul that have been closed off to reality in order to begin the restorative healing to bring us back to Jesus. Even more so, He wants the guilt we harbor, the thoughts which torment us from the past, to flee our heads in order to be replaced with what He fulfilled on the cross. He never expected for sin to disappear but He did show us that death can be conquered by unconditional sacrificial love which emerges by loving our self first. Even in the times our decisions have been the "kiss" which handed Him over to be crucified.

So again what was Jesus' ultimate reaction when He looked at Judas in the Garden? After He predicted who would betray Him and then watching His beloved friend call Him out to the soldiers he was handing Him over to, Christ simply looked at Judas with pity. A sympathy for what Judas had become, not merely because of greed, but because he was so weak, the devil used him as a pawn. Jesus did not speak one ill thing of Judas that night, only staring at him empathetically for the inner torment that would eventually drive him to suicide once the Savior was in custody.

Based on understanding how much Christ wants to extend mercy through the Eucharist and in prayer, it's important we discuss the Sacramental component and gift that makes all of our healing possible. While forgiveness is an integral part of Jesus' presence when we fully receive Him in the Eucharist, we must understand the necessity for the Sacrament of Reconciliation to remain at the forefront of our healing.

There is a difference between reconciliation and forgiveness. For this reason, it's vital for us to partake in the Sacrament of Reconciliation prior to receiving the gift of the Eucharist. To be fully restored in communion with God. All those whom had their sins admonished by the living God still needed to continue to rehabilitate themselves spiritually by maintaining a life connected with Christ. This was the key component Judas couldn't see as possible for his actions while on Earth. As with everything else which relates back to God, we underestimate the unending mercy He wants to extend to each of us.

> *During his public life Jesus not only forgave sins, but also made plain the effect of this forgiveness: he reintegrated forgiven sinners into the community of the People of God from which sin had alienated or even excluded them. A remarkable sign of this is the fact that Jesus receives sinners at his table, a gesture that expresses in an astonishing way both God's forgiveness and the return to the bosom of the People of God. (CCC 1443)*

Over the years, this Sacrament of Healing as I would call it has been set aside by most. "I have talked with God and He forgives me, so I am good. I don't have to tell my sins to a priest who is just a sinner like me." Phrases like this are usually offered when people talk about going to confession. It is this level of thinking that results with only ten to fifteen confessions being heard a week in parishes with thousands of parishioners. A large number of people who are not fully realizing the grace of God. We come forth for His love to be poured out on us at Mass despite showing up holding the same whip the guards did as they stood at the cross staring at the man who gave everything for His people. But He just didn't die to only forgive; He gave Himself so we would know the path to Heaven. Reconciliation offers the grace filled healing we aren't necessarily able to recognize when we simply ask for forgiveness from God one on one.

While finding Jesus' forgiveness in the Eucharist is both a model to forgive and accept forgiveness, we must also be aware of the pathway that allows us to be worthy of the love He offers unconditionally to heal us. An intense journey examining who we are, what we have done wrong and how we make things right which allow us to be open to what we are receiving. We take the steps that lead us to His feet to be forgiven, understand the sins we have committed against Him and see the times we chose something worldly and less than holy over the ultimate relationship He wants to have with us. In this manner, not only is the Eucharist our source and summit for ultimate healing, it is the embodiment of resurrected Christ made whole because love was bigger than hate. An opportunity to see ourselves how He sees us no matter if we are brought to Him by others, saved from condemnation of the world or forgiven in spite of our most serious offense. We are unconditionally forgiven and made whole with Him through the Eucharist.

# SHARING THE JOURNEY:

*How can there be so much peace amidst the chaos? Doesn't the world see what His power can do to make us see only love? A world of problems, an environment of in-fighting and hurt everywhere abounds. Yet when I sit with my Lord, everything ceases and tranquility reigns supreme. All for nothing other than sitting and being still with Him!*

*Lord I would rather glorify you in truth, then to receive praise from the world for sin.*

# PRAYER:

*Lord Jesus, please forgive me for the sins I have committed and the ways I have withheld forgiveness from those who have hurt me. In this moment, I pray for your healing powers to wash over me and those I have hurt so I am able to receive your grace in Holy Communion.*

# Reflection

_____

_____

_____

_____

_____

_____

_____

_____

_____

_____

_____

_____

_____

_____

# VII

## TENDING THE SHEEP
LEADERSHIP VALUES & RESPONSIBILITY

---

*"Our sharing in the Body and Blood of
Christ has no other purpose than to
transform us into that which we receive."*
*~Pope St. Leo the Great*

---

Receiving the model to be a servant leader is one of the most practical gifts we find in the Eucharist to apply to our daily living. There is no way around our call and how we are to lead, guide and care for those entrusted to us. Jesus, the ultimate leader and shepherd continually showed us why the flock never desired to stray from His presence. Christ was a methodical, compassionate, patient leader who possessed the skills of communication which helped people grow in whatever role or position they held. Never to belittle, rather correct. Not looking to hold back but to lift up. His followers always found reasons to hope when all seemed lost and trusted in teachings they couldn't understand.

> The Word became flesh to be our model of holi-
> ness: "Take my yoke upon you, and learn from me." "I am
> the way, and the truth, and the life; no one comes to the
> Father, but by me." On the mountain of the Transfigura-
> tion, the Father commands: "Listen to him!" Jesus is the
> model for the Beatitudes and the norm of the new law:
> "Love one another as I have loved you." This love implies
> an effective offering of oneself, after his example.
> (CCC 459)

As we pray for skills and worldly outcomes of the work we are doing, it becomes necessary to remain rooted in Christ's presence to allow our labors to culminate in grace filled results. By finding this aspect of Jesus through the Eucharist we are reminded who we ultimately serve when we consume Him. Regardless of our position, career or title, we are as much the servant to Christ as He is to us.

Take the final time Jesus gathered with His disciples as their leader: The Last Supper. In our humanness, if we were going away, we would feel like we have a million things to tell those we lead and give them all their final instructions. This isn't what we hear about in scripture. How does Jesus teach them a final lesson?

> "Fully aware that the Father had put everything into his
> power and that he had come from God and was return-
> ing to God, he rose from supper and took off his outer
> garments. He took a towel and tied it around his
> waist. Then he poured water into a basin and began to
> wash the disciples' feet and dry them with the towel
> around his waist. He came to Simon Peter, who said to
> him, "Master, are you going to wash my feet?" Jesus an-
> swered and said to him, "What I am doing, you do not

*understand now, but you will understand later,"*
*(Jn 13:3-7)*

His leadership was found in the service He offered to those He loved; those whom He was entrusting His entire church. Christ's, leadership wasn't about having to make Himself respected as "the boss" by wielding His power. Instead, Jesus gave them the ultimate example by doing something they didn't understand or fully grasp in the moment. By this example, we can come to lead all those we shepherd by not always being the one talking but by being the doer of what we believe. This applies all the way from parenting to being the CEO of a Fortune 500 company. Show others by your living example that the process to fulfillment is about something bigger they may not always comprehend.

In any group, ministry or corporation, a leader filled with only words without servant values will become "*a noisy gong or a clanging cymbal.*" (1 Cor 13:1) So when we come to Him to hold Him in our hands, the towel is still wrapped around His waist so He can serve you if you allow Him. Are those entrusted to you being served by you in the same way? This is the humility it takes to be not only a great leader, but one who shepherds in the image of Christ. The best decisions we can make for our people are the ones which don't place the burden back on them, but rather they allow us to take the helm quietly and confidently to guide them.

James Hind, author of *The Heart and Soul of Effective Management* states: "There is a gap between the church altar and the company boardroom." However, it's not just the boardroom, it's also our family dining rooms and even our church conference rooms. Living our faith out in our homes, communities and workplace is part of our call to evangelize outside of Sunday Mass. Often times though, we're not sure where to draw the strength from to be courageous enough to do so. We're uncomfortable blurring the line of sharing our beliefs with people who could possibly consider it taboo to discuss faith anywhere else other than inside a church. Jesus certainly knew what it was like to be challenged for conveying the truth. In the Eucharist we receive His leadership attributes that certainly gave others the trust and courage to follow Him in His ministry despite the world.

In analyzing all the ways Jesus led we have to place an intense focus on scripture. After all, this would be His "corporate file" if we were going to have HR give Him a full review. Nonetheless, it's an important journey for us to take as leaders because it allows us to do what the Bible intends for us to do: place ourselves in the story. Allowing it to measure the manner in which we live our lives, while inspiring us to work towards success while maintaining integrity.

In life we tend to place a distance between our faith and our places of business or school. We place what we believe at an arms-length so others won't question us. Even in our homes we might be on different paths of our faith journey or even varying beliefs. If we happen to be the one in charge for a corporation, the decisions we can be forced to make are sometimes outside of the moral compass our faith calls us to base all our actions on. Ironically, we can even fall victim to separation from Christ within the leadership of our various ministries within the church. Our arguments can become about who "owns the coffee cups used for funeral luncheons or pancake breakfasts," rather than the aspect of community being built when the paper products are being used. The heart of the matter comes to light that our coming to the Eucharist fuels our soul to connect with the leadership skills Christ possessed. Jesus corrected others humbly, He proved His point sternly and most importantly, He led others to excellence.

We are faced with choosing to do what is best and right over what might be easiest or even most profitable. We can never lose sight of the work we do and our gifts are only on loan from God. Just as Jesus always remained obedient to the Father, we too must remember it is never about us. Christ knew the work he was doing here was only temporary and it was merely to lead others to Heaven, not just to simply worship the person of Jesus the Nazarene. Our victories should be for the common good for all people to better the world in which we live. In the times we begin to lose sight of this, we must return to Christ in prayer and the Eucharist to allow Him to increase so we might decrease (Jn 3:30).

> In keeping with the social nature of man, the good of each individual is necessarily related to the common good, which in turn can be defined only in reference to the human person: Do not live entirely isolated, having retreated into yourselves, as if you were already justified, but gather instead to seek the common good together. (CCC 1905)

When we look at our own lives and reflect on the greatest leaders who have influenced us, we see traits in them that become part of us. So to it was with Jesus learning from Joseph, as the leader of the house, St. Joseph surely handed down traits, which would have taught a young Jesus how to handle Himself when He was with others. Jesus would have seen a man who remained obedient to the will of God without question. Whenever an order was handed down, Joseph remained faithful to God to follow His plan while leading his family to safety. I can only imagine the talks they must have engaged in. It was part of Joseph's role to help a young Jesus grow into a man. We can assume the influence must have been strong because others identified Jesus with Joseph. *"Isn't that the carpenter's son?"* (Mt. 13:55) They asked as Jesus preached. As a father, Joseph's role would not have been easy, but He remained true to his faith and helped Jesus become a leader because of the example He had from the man who loved him so deeply.

Unconditionally bringing Christ into the world through our life outside of the church should be our goal instead of downplaying what our belief in Him means. Through a "service based" leadership role, we can always put the image of Jesus before others. In the process, we will be reminded daily who we have become because He died for us on the cross. Not just to die, but to once more lead by sacrifice. When this happens it changes everything about how we work to lead others. Not only are we working to reach certain milestones or simply be profitable but we are doing our part to create better people.

Think about it, because you led with the heart of Christ found in your faith through the Eucharist, you have the ability to help create better parents, stronger families, morally based companies and even convert hearts for those who want to know your ultimate secret to success. As Fr. James Martin recounted in a Forbes Magazine interview, "Jesus laid out an idea of what the world could be like – which he called the "reign of God" – where the hungry would be fed, the naked clothed, the sick healed and the dead raised — which electrified his listeners. And inspired them to work for that vision."

Receiving Jesus as the leader who served until death will assist all our efforts to grow in love while contributing to a new generation of believers who want to follow Christ because of the way we put His love on display outside of church. Don't just allow Christ to be the one you follow for an hour on Sunday, let Him shepherd you so you can lead others with a servant's heart stemming from the ultimate respect shared in the Eucharist.

> *"Remain in me, as I remain in you. Just as a branch cannot bear fruit on its own unless it remains on the vine, so neither can you unless you remain in me. I am the vine, you are the branches. Whoever remains in me and I in him will bear much fruit, because without me you can do nothing." (Jn 15:4-5)*

# SHARING THE JOURNEY:

*Lord let me continue to be courageous. In a world who longs to rob us of you, give me strength to ALWAYs be the light who proves everything we desire is found in you. Knowing there will be challenges and times of struggle, do not let fear overtake the courage you provide me as a child of God.*

*I lay it down tonight... each chain link, each shackle, every weight that not allowed me to run to the Lord for strength. Let me lead as Christ did, with a calm nature and a gentle hand.*

# PRAYER:

*Jesus you were truly the ultimate leader. I pray to receive all of the traits you displayed while shepherding those you walked with. Help me be the best servant leader I can be for those you have entrusted in my care. Give me the grace to remain humble with my gifts, appreciative of my talents and steadfast in my resolve to do what is right for the common good of all.*

# Reflection

# VIII

# HIS EYES
## A REFLECTION OF LOVE & COMPASSION

---

*"How many of you say: I should like to see His face, His garments, His shoes. You do see Him, you touch Him, you eat Him. He gives Himself to you, not only that you may see Him, but also to be your food and nourishment." ~St. John Chrysostom*

---

A major fallacy we can fall victim to is thinking that unless we are physically able to be the hands and feet of Christ for people, then we are not doing all we can to help others. This would be like saying, "The only way we know someone loves us is because there is some physical touch that occurs to make us feel their love." False, it can be as simple as the look in our eyes which shares more than a thousand words ever could and or a disingenuous holding of hands could add. The eyes have the ability to add a level of sincerity immediately recognizable, which places our heart on display. There is beauty through daily interactions which require no words at all; when our simple encounters with others allow them to see the eyes of Christ within us.

In uniting with Christ through the Eucharist, we possess the grace to move beyond merely being His hands and feet. We become His eyes for the rest of the world to see Him through us. An attribute which also allows us to see everything differently as He did. Every glance at a stranger, a longing gaze for a lover or the tenderness in a stare to show compassion to a child is a reflection of His unconditional love. It's our witness that inspires others, sharing hope with all we meet. As Christ said, "*Whoever has seen me has seen the Father.*" (Jn 14:9) We continue to keep this alive today.

Scripture gives us accounts where it took nothing from Jesus but His presence and gentle nature to heal others around him. On the way to the cross "*A large crowd of people followed Jesus, including many women who mourned and lamented him. Jesus turned to them and said, 'Daughters of Jerusalem, do not weep for me; weep instead for yourselves and for your children.'*" (Lk 23:27-28) How much hurt do we encounter in a day? How many have been placed on our path with worry or anxiety who need us to look on them kindly? Jesus' presence in the Eucharist calls us to be aware of those moments as He was. Even in one of His weakest moments (physically) He is still thinking about who He can comfort.

In another instance, the story of the woman suffering from a hemorrhage gives us insight of how our faith to believe in who Jesus is offers us power when it causes Him to look kindly upon us.

*A woman suffering hemorrhages for twelve years came up behind him and touched the tassel on his cloak. She said to herself, "If only I can touch his cloak, I shall be cured." Jesus turned around and saw her, and said, "Courage, daughter! Your faith has saved you." And from that hour the woman was cured. (Mt. 9:20-22)*

Even amidst feeling lost in the crowd and without human hope for a cure, it took her faith and Christ's recognition of that faith to heal her immediately. In the times our faces blend in with the rest of society and we feel no one knows our pain, Christ is there through others looking upon us. Physically He is unable to lay hands on us but by seeking those who reflect His eyes, we find comfort and open ourselves up to be fully healed. If we can't settle for anything less than to stare into His eyes, He waits in the tabernacle of our churches so that all we need to do is look upon Him with our request so He can see our faith. In the days where we cannot seem to get going or our bodies are too broken to complete a task we still have the ability to share Christ with others through our eyes while we carry our daily cross.

Looking back at us in the Eucharist is the person of Jesus Christ who sees right into our soul. An unconditional love which knows our heart, our struggles, our pain. While He cannot physically embrace us in that moment, it's this connection that provides an electric feeling of euphoria in our bodies as we approach Him. No words are necessary, no touch could compare to what the eyes can tell us as we walk up to receive Him.

Revelation 1:14 tells us, "...his eyes were like blazing fire." I can only imagine burning with love and passion for justice. A justice which includes those He loves who longed to be with Him. As we walk down the aisle, approaching Jesus in the Eucharist, He gazes at us much longer than we return the stare. Often we are distracted by the moment of waiting in line or wondering what traffic will be like. One could even say He watches us with an expectation of joy that we are willing to come to His table to receive everything He wants to give us. If we looked close enough and could imagine the tender mercy found in this gaze, we would certainly know He is accepting us unconditionally because He loved us first. This is the same reflection of authentic love and complete healing He gave to so many while walking the Earth. Likewise, once He is part of us we serve as a reflection to share those eyes with the rest of the world. Finding ourselves lost in the work of Christ goes far beyond action; it is also the manner in which we portray the sincerity we desire to do the deed.

To give you a living example relative to the power found in "His eyes," I offer you the following personal encounter. To date, I've had two transfiguration moments in my life. When I say "transfiguration," I mean I literally saw Christ in His physical state through another person; as plane as you see the people around you. I could never really put it into words which would do either of them justice, but in sharing one of them it might enlighten your heart for the moments He is presenting Himself to you through the eyes of another person. For me, it was about giving me the gift of courage to face something I never could foresee. As I would later learn, my lack of understanding closely mirrored the way the disciples most likely felt during Christ's transfiguration on the mountain. (Mt 17:1-8)

*Christ's Transfiguration aims at strengthening the
apostles' faith in anticipation of his Passion: the ascent
on to the "high mountain" prepares for the ascent to Calvary. Christ, Head of the Church, manifests what his Body
contains and radiates in the sacraments: "the hope of
glory" (Col 1:27; cf.: St. Leo the Great, Sermon 51, 3: PL
54, 310C). (CCC 568)*

It happened to be during an apathetic state of mind during
Mass in which I was witness to one of the most beautiful vi-
sions a human being could ever receive. I was fulfilling an
obligation as part of my role as emcee for a local event in
Cleveland, OH called the FEST. I was assigned to a parish
where I was offering invites at all Masses to get parishioners
excited about event. After five Masses in a weekend, I reserved myself to the fact that the last one would be just another Liturgy that would have my role come after communion ended. I planned on just playing my "part" and then
heading home.

During mass, as the priest prepared to proclaim The Word
of the God, the entire congregation stood to sing the "Alle-
luia." A little strawberry blonde, blue eyed, precious toddler
was being held upright in her mother's arms in the pew directly in front of me. As I sang the little girl began to mouth
the words along with me. I gently smiled back at her as she
innocently looked back at me. In an instant, her look
changed from the child seen by all into the face of our living
God, Jesus Christ, right in front of me. Astonished, I became
weak in the knees and breathless.

What began as an ordinary moment of me looking into a
young girls' eyes, suddenly it became a gateway for Christ to
prepare my heart for something I could never imagine. This

three to five second encounter (which literally felt like eternity) to see Him before me was surreal. Although, its true purpose was really meant to serve as a reassurance (preparation) I would fall back on months later when I returned to do a family presentation at this particular parish.

Fast forward five months to February 27, 2012. It was six days before my scheduled event at St. Mary's in Chardon, OH. Life changed forever for the entire area when a school shooting occurred at Chardon High School across the street from St. Mary's Church. When it was over, five students were shot. Three were pronounced dead: Russel King Jr., Demetrius Hewlin and Daniel Parmertor. A senseless act of school violence had robbed this community of their innocence. The three funerals would be held at St. Mary's. One on the day before I was scheduled to present and the other two, over the days immediately following. I figured their healing would need to begin by someone other than myself. After all, how could I possibly be the person who could help? I was wrong.

Fearful. Doubting and filled with sorrow, I sobbed the remainder of the day as details were continuously pouring in on the news. Those tears would stay with me most of that week. The school was only thirty minutes from my house and with two school aged children, it was too close to home. I literally prayed that I would not have to go and stand before people who knew hurt in a way I couldn't comprehend. For the first time I questioned my role in God's ministry.

Two days after the shooting, I received a call that the parish still wanted to go ahead with the event I was offering for freshman Confirmation candidates and their parents. The actual words spoken by the Director of Religious Education to me on the phone were, "I prayed to God that He would send us the right person to help us heal, and he said He was sending you." I remained overwhelmed with fear of not being worthy of the role I was being asked to play in all this. Then I remembered back to that moment when Christ presented himself to me on that August day at mass in the same church.

The eyes of that child leading to the transformation of Christ in front me assured me I was not alone. Strengthened by the Eucharist but reminded by the innocent eyes of a Child who allowed Christ to shine through. I was given the courage I needed to present God's intended message to those who needed once again find to Christ through pain while not losing hope. He knew His plan for me long before I could ever imagine it and it was His eyes that gave me the ultimate strength I needed.

While I have sometimes tried to talk myself out of what I saw that day, I know it's truth. Besides what my eyes saw, there has never been a burning on my heart like that instance since. Even my wife who happened to be sitting next to me saw a change in my demeanor the instant it occurred.

One of the most amazing things about this particular moment with Christ was after mass ended when I told the mother of the little girl what happened. Instead of looking at me like I was crazy, she looked back at me as we stood in the gathering area and simply said, "Oh, her name is Faustina and this happens all the time." So, if you ever are blessed to share in a moment like this, my only advice is, never question or try to dismiss the reality; it's just the way

Christ works.

In the same manner we have found Jesus in the Eucharist, we must be His image for all those who may never set foot into a church building. If we inspire them through our simple demeanor, with His eyes, the look they see will be that of the risen Christ which may cause a conversion they have never gone through before. Most of the work we can do to bring Jesus' love to others will statistically be with people we will never meet or physically touch ever.

Being the eyes of Christ is a gift we can offer at any time. From the grocery store, to places of work, to our churches - offering a look toward another filled with His compassionate, caring eyes brings them closer to Him without speaking a single phrase. These brief moments of consideration offer a glimpse into who we are because of the love found through our Catholic faith. If others begin to know His love through your kindhearted look, its impact might just lead them back to His Kingdom.

> Christ's disciples are to conform themselves to him until
> he is formed in them (cf. Gal 4:19). "For this reason we,
> who have been made like to him, who have died with him
> and risen with him, are taken up into the mysteries of his
> life, until we reign together with him" (LG 7 § 4).
> (CCC 562)

Likewise, His eyes are everywhere looking upon us. The same eyes we receive in Him at the altar, so we may become transformed to share them with the world. No matter what age you are, physical talents you have been blessed with, you can offer peace, love and joy to the world by being the eyes of Christ to those around you. Consuming Him to be His reflection for all. Being His eyes, doesn't take time, it won't cost you a cent and there is no special talent needed except for a willingness to let Him shine through you. When our eyes become His eyes, unconditionally, it changes us by the people we let see Him through our presence. The eyes of Christ found in the Eucharist are not bound to human sight. So you cannot simply confine them to working to only "see" with His eyes, but rather being His eyes for the rest of the world so He can be "seen" through you as well.

# SHARING THE JOURNEY:

*Allow me to be a light bright enough for others to believe just through my actions.*

*What does it mean to be the image Christ? It is all encompassing to not only love but to be peace, to forgive, to have been and be knocked down but still proclaim truth. It is to be all of Him as He is to us. So the question is, what do you want from Him? Which will yield exactly what you should be for others.*

# PRAYER:

*Lord allow me to receive your eyes through your divine presence in the Eucharist so I may be your light for the world. May I never forget the power my demeanor and presence can offer a world who longs to know you. I am always a reflection of You. I also pray to see things as you would see them so I can better understand those in need and find the ones lost and hurting.*

# Reflection

_____

_____

_____

_____

_____

_____

_____

_____

_____

_____

_____

_____

_____

_____

_____

# IX

# THE GARDEN TO
# THE CROSS
## REMAINING OBEDIENCT TO GOD'S PLAN

---

*"If we but paused for a moment to consider attentively what takes place in this Sacrament, I am sure that the thought of Christ's love for us would transform the coldness of our hearts into a fire of love and gratitude." --St. Angela of Foligno*

---

One hurdle so many of us struggle during our faith journey that causes us to falter more often than we acknowledge: "Acceptance." Not acceptance of ourselves as we've talked about before, but now embracing things as God needs them. Surrendering to God's overall plan with unconditional acceptance when we're fearful, lost or feeling like we can't continue on can seem impossible. Jesus' endurance found throughout all aspects of "The Passion" takes Him from the Garden to the Cross, an obedience that fulfills His sacrifice found in the Eucharist. It gives us hope that through the gift of His surrender, we will be filled with the grace to journey on when we think we can't continue on.

In our case it might come in the form of lamenting questions like "Why?" or "How?" Possibly it comes to a head in times we would rather give up than continue on with uncertainty. These are the moments we need to find Christ's amazing gift of acceptance that exists in every aspect of the Eucharist. Jesus didn't merely die a natural death and became the Bread of Life. He willingly allowed His Father's will to be fulfilled in the proper manner to become the source of life we receive over and over during communion. In receiving Him, He extends a reassurance within us that He knows exactly how hard things might get. Nonetheless, He reminds us that the beauty of fulfillment through His Father is definitely worth the struggle at any given moment.

We would view Christ's passion and death as purely tragic if it doesn't have anything to do with faith. A man crucified because of what he preached. A gentle healer made to suffer for giving others hope and aiding those in need. However, in our belief, no matter what happened during Jesus' life, His life would have meant nothing without the Cross. He was sent by the Father to die for our sins. Living proof of His obedience, courage and commitment to do what God needed rather than what He wanted.

His humanness is bravely put on display from the moment He accepts His fate once again in the Garden of Gethsemane through His entire road to Calvary culminating in His last breath on the Cross.

> *"For as by one man's disobedience many were made sin-*
> *ners, so by one man's obedience many will be made*
> *righteous." By his obedience unto death, Jesus accom-*
> *plished the substitution of the suffering Servant, who*
> *"makes himself an offering for sin", when "he bore the*
> *sin of many", and who "shall make many to be accounted*
> *righteous", for "he shall bear their iniquities". Jesus*
> *atoned for our faults and made satisfaction for our sins*
> *to the Father. (CCC 615)*

One of the most humbling moments in reading the passion in our Gospels is when Jesus Christ, true God and true man, *"was in such agony and he prayed so fervently that his sweat became like drops of blood falling on the ground."* (Lk 22:44) What brings this about? Fear. Here is the Son of Man who can only fulfill His purpose on Earth by dying for our sins, which He professed throughout His entire ministry, but still He becomes so scared of the final trial that His human emotions take over to question the Father's will for Him. So why did Christ have such agony? The Baltimore Catechism (#375) outlined them as:

> *It is believed Our Lord's agony in the garden was caused:*
>
> - *By his clear knowledge of all He was*
>   *soon to endure;*
> - *By the sight of the many offenses com-*
>   *mitted against His Father by the sins*
>   *of the whole world;*
> - *By His knowledge of men's ingratitude*
>   *for the blessings of redemption.*

His prayers end with Him unconditionally accepting what must be done for the greater good; a call shared by all of us each day.

Face it, we want what we want. We pray for what we want. We ultimately work for what we want. Putting ourselves third (behind God and family) to do what the Father wants is not always top on our priority list. Stepping forth to receive the Eucharist and finding Christ's acceptance of God's will is the nourishment for the soul we need to remain fervent to do exactly that. The Passion contained within the Eucharist models what it means to live a life of vocation which places our Father and those we love before ourselves.

So how do we accomplish acceptance as Christ did? Learning to surrender means to literally place ourselves in a vulnerable yet reverent position. Once again, we examine Christ in the Garden at His most difficult moment. The demeanor in which He is praying: on His knees. *"He advanced a little and fell prostrate in prayer, saying, "My Father, if it is possible, let this cup pass from me; yet, not as I will, but as you will."* (Mt 26:39) This is the same position we head back to our pew, or seat, to ultimately surrender ourselves to search for our own ability to give all of ourselves to Him. This moment connects us through the Eucharist to the entire story of the Passion ending with Christ offering His body for us. His body endured the whip marks for our sins, the weight of the cross for our struggles and ultimately the holes violently created with nails and a spear, all wounds through which He poured Himself out for us. The story He surrendered to acceptance.

The Garden isn't just the place where Jesus displayed fear of His purpose or where He found lack of discipline in His disciples who could not stay awake. It's the place Christ asks us to be vigilant in order to remain steadfast despite the moments everything seems hopeless. A demeanor found deep within the Eucharist that calls us to prepare even in the dark night. A time where things still may not go our way, but we allow ourselves to be handed over so we can be made anew through dying to ourselves. Our own personal Good Friday leading us to an Easter Sunday.

While the story of The Passion begins in the Garden, we know it ends on the Cross. The bible gives us intimate details of the tremendous suffering Christ endured while walking the long roads to Calvary. For when He prayed these words again, *"My Father, if it is not possible that this cup pass without my drinking it, your will be done!"* (Mt 26:42) It meant humiliation would be an aspect of mockery to which so many would deny the King. The scourging, His falling, the crowning of thorns and eventually, the nailing to the cross were all filled with acts of hatred for a man who had done nothing except look to lead others with love to the Father. Still, He carried His cross for you and I, making sure nothing would stop Him short of what was necessary to complete His journey.

Even after His strength placed Him on those wooden beams so we might be made whole, fear continued to flow from Jesus' lips as a result of the unimaginable pain running through His body. *"My God, my God, why have you forsaken me?"* (Mt.27:46) mirrored Psalm 22:2, *"My God, my God, why have you abandoned me?"* Not only does this show us He held sorrow in His heart for the separation our sins may have caused Him to feel from His Father, but rather His faithfulness to recite a passage He would have learned as a little boy forming His own faith in the Temple. One of many examples of what it means to remain faithful despite being in agony.

So, yes, we receive the sacrificed Christ who was led away in the dark of the night from the Garden. In His passion, the broken, battered and crucified Servant is placed onto our tongues so He may once again take on the sins we have committed and He can redeem our souls. There we place Him a new tomb which He awaits us to share the resurrected Lord with the world through our actions. A chance for us to unconditionally show others that our Savior gave us a model of hope despite struggling through human fear and prejudices of others which resulted in murdering an innocent man. It then becomes our role, on our knees, to pray for the Father's will with full knowledge nothing will ever be done to us that will not be glorified. If we can always return to our faith based roots, love will win. However, none of it will be accomplished without our unconditional surrender to acceptance that will defeat fear of the unknown. Finding Jesus' acceptance in the Eucharist gives each of us the courage to know Easter Sunday is not far despite the turmoil of Good Friday.

# SHARING THE JOURNEY:

*He places my hand on His chest while we sit in the Garden. His hour has not come but He has chosen me as a special disciple to reveal all to. We talk, He is calm, He knows it is coming but the fear has not hit Him. Jesus, I can feel emptiness already, I begin to display sadness and anger in that moment I feel the love of His heart grow, the tenderness radiates into my body and the understanding to settle into my brain. This is truth, and there truly is NO other way. He expresses once more that without us to carry His church, the world will never truly know. I commit myself in that moment, accepting trails and grace to honor Him and lead others HOME.*

*I see Lord that I am humbled in my defeats and in my own personal "crucifixions." Let me always gain the same strength and story of victory as you did the day you experienced torment, teasing and denial, even though you spoke the truth.*

# PRAYER:

*Lord Jesus you remained obedient to death. Some days I struggle to remain obedient to things that simply make me uncomfortable. I pray to overcome my own selfish wants and walk the path necessary to fulfill God's plan for me on this Earth. When I receive you're your Passion in the Eucharist, allow me to understand all my crosses have a purpose and I will never be left to journey alone.*

# REFLECTION

# X

# ON THE THIRD DAY
## HOPE IN THE RESURRECTION

---

*"Just as bread from the earth, when it receives the invocation of God, is no longer common bread but the Eucharist, made up of two elements, one earthly and one heavenly, so also our bodies, in receiving the Eucharist, are no longer corruptible, for they have the hope of resurrection,"*
~ St. Irenaeus

---

Have you really ever thought about the fact that not only are you finding the Christ who offered Himself for us on the Cross, but you are also consuming the risen Lord who defeated death on Easter Sunday? We tend to concentrate solely on the sacrifice of Christ as we prepare and receive the Eucharist. We know His suffering, but we also must not forget His glorification. It is the risen Christ which sets our heart on fire. It is not the broken and beaten body of Christ which lives and creates within us, it is the resurrected radiant Lord who gives light wherever we go. A mark on your soul that humbly says "He is with us in our hearts each and every moment of every day."

> By the consecration the transubstantiation of the bread and wine into the Body and Blood of Christ is brought about. Under the consecrated species of bread and wine Christ himself, living and glorious, is present in a true, real, and substantial manner: his Body and his Blood, with his soul and his divinity (cf. Council of Trent: DS 1640; 1651). (CCC 1413)

In Mass, we can allow the words of the consecration during the Eucharistic Prayer to place our focus on the foretelling of what was about to happen during the Last Supper. While the Eucharist is associated with the suffering and complete giving of Jesus on the Cross, we are receiving the complete story of Salvation history and fulfillment of the Scriptures that conclude with His rising from the dead. By running to Christ in the Supper of the Lord, we are finding a resurrected Jesus who sets our hearts on fire for Him because we are able to recognize Him fully and completely.

To only focus on individual aspects of Christ at any time, causes us to miss opportunities to see Him in the world. We place limitations on His divinity, missing the moments He is presenting Himself to us so we will remain open to His love. Are we able to recognize or notice the risen Christ when He appears in our midst? Taking the Eucharist for granted in a way where we do not see Jesus visible beyond the host can keep us from the encounter that gives fullness to what we believe. We are reminded of this through the two disciples who came upon the resurrected Christ on the road to

## Emmaus.

*Now that very day two of them were going to a village seven miles from Jerusalem called Emmaus, and they were conversing about all the things that had occurred. And it happened that while they were conversing and debating, Jesus himself drew near and walked with them, but their eyes were prevented from recognizing him. He asked them, "What are you discussing as you walk along?" They stopped, looking downcast. One of them, named Cleopas, said to him in reply, "Are you the only visitor to Jerusalem who does not know of the things that have taken place there in these days?" And he replied to them, "What sort of things?" They said to him, "The things that happened to Jesus the Nazarene, who was a prophet mighty in deed and word before God and all the people, how our chief priests and rulers both handed him over to a sentence of death and crucified him. But we were hoping that he would be the one to redeem Israel; and besides all this, it is now the third day since this took place. Some women from our group, however, have astounded us: they were at the tomb early in the morning and did not find his body; they came back and reported that they had indeed seen a vision of angels who announced that he was alive. Then some of those with us went to the tomb and found things just as the women had described, but him they did not see." And he said to them, "Oh, how foolish you are! How slow of heart to believe all that the prophets spoke! Was it not necessary that the Messiah should suffer these things and enter into his glory?" Then beginning with Moses and all the prophets, he interpreted to them what referred to him in all the scriptures. As they approached the village to which they were going, he gave the impression that he was going on farther. But they urged him, "Stay with us, for it is nearly evening and the day is almost over." So he went in to stay with them. And it happened that, while he was with them at table, he took bread, said the blessing, broke it, and gave it to them. With that their eyes were opened and they recognized him, but he vanished from their sight. Then they said to each other, "Were not our hearts burning [within us] while he spoke to us on the way and opened the scriptures to us?" So they set out at once and returned to Jerusalem where they found gathered together the eleven and those with them who were saying, "The Lord has truly been raised and has appeared to Simon!" Then the two recounted what had taken place on the way and how he was made known to them in the breaking of the bread. (Lk 24:13-25)*

I chose to include this entire passage for some important reasons. So many pieces of it are related to what we sometimes lose sight of as Catholic Christians receiving the Eucharist. If we don't find ourselves receiving the resurrected Christ, then there is no hope. Our hearts would have to be fulfilled by the actions which led to His death instead of the promise found only through Him conquering death. Our belief in Him allows us to live forever with Him. A promised granted unconditionally through our desire to recognize Him.

Initially, the disciples weren't 100% sure what was going to happen now that they "lost" Jesus. On the journey to Emmaus, walking next to Jesus on the road they didn't notice their Master. Their fear and grief gave up on the hope Christ promised and they stopped looking beyond themselves. It is only after He shares the Eucharist in the breaking of the bread, they realize it was Christ who walked WITH them. In disbelief they look at each other saying "Were not your hearts burning within us while he spoke to us on the way and opened the scriptures to us." They are disappointed and beating themselves up thinking "He has given us everything and we can't even recognize him." How often are you downplaying the feeling of elation that comes through the awesome things that God does for you when He is right there next to you in your life? Especially every time we find Jesus in the Eucharist presenting Himself for each one of us. We need to display the confidence of what we believe in a manner that others know we trust beyond doubt in the faith we hold. In a sense we are given this gift that things fall apart so they can fall back together. Broken and blessed, but made whole and new; even better.

Jesus really is the answer for all our hopes; we need to trust him no matter what. The Eucharist is the Word made flesh and it renews our minds and ignites our hearts! Just like the disciples on the road who were able to recognize Jesus only after they dined with Him. To receive Him recalls we see this differently and begin to notice Him in places we didn't before. What can we do to deepen our relationship to know Him all the time and not to deny this amazing relationship? We cannot hide a "Heart that is On Fire" because the light it radiates is too bright for those around us to ignore. Just as it says in Psalm 119:105, *"Thy Word is a lamp unto my feet and a light unto my path."* We are the ones who have to illuminate the way for others. It is the resurrected Christ we take out into the world.

Each of us is called to be a disciple for the Lord. We are baptized Priest, Prophet and King as the waters are poured over our head and oils anoint us as His children; Holy ones. Finding a heart on fire in the Eucharist is the beautiful aspect of loving, living and forgiving like Christ. The resurrected Jesus, who fans the flame within us to know what we believe is true. We are the vessels of all He fulfilled during His time on Earth. A journey which led Him to sit at the right hand of the Father where He reigns over us. The Sacrament we get to celebrate is our chance to see Him as often as we wish to know He remains with us still. A chance to receive all of Him glorified in the resurrection.

> Not only that, but we even boast of our afflictions, know-ing that affliction produces endurance, and endurance, proven character, and proven character, hope, and hope does not disappoint, because the love of God has been poured out into our hearts through the holy Spirit that has been given to us. (Rom 5:3-5)

In the most Holy Sacrament of the Eucharist we receive the same hearts on fire which the Lord sets ablaze for us to no-tice Him far beyond the moment He comes to us in com-munion. It melts away our inadequacies while lighting the path for us toward true discipleship. Let's allow our own commitment to set our hearts on fire enabling us to pro-claim and live with belief, faith and hope in the midst of dif-ficult and uncertain times. Someday, somewhere, your problems will be bigger than anything on this Earth can help you with it's vital we can rely on our conversations with Christ in the Eucharist to help us get through them. His un-conditional resurrection contained within the host is the an-swer for all our hopes.

> The risen Christ lives in the hearts of his faithful while they await that fulfillment. In Christ, Christians "have tasted.... the powers of the age to come and their lives are swept up by Christ into the heart of divine life, so that they may "live no longer for themselves but for him who for their sake died and was raised. (CCC 655)

Having tasted of His presence, it's up to us to decide if we are going to journey on a path for us to go deeper. How do we go deeper in our lives? What truly sets our hearts on fire? Do we take this body and blood and transform our lives? Does it set our hearts on fire? Jesus wants us to know Him and have a close personal fellowship with Him by dining together.

The resurrected Christ also shares with us the precious encounters of continual teaching he offered the Apostles till His final ascension into Heaven. Times which they still broke bread together and the physical state of how He revealed Himself brought comfort at their low points.

We must never forget the relationship we have with Jesus through the promises He fulfilled by rising on the third day. Finding Jesus in the Eucharist allows us to see beyond the suffering of any given moment, unconditional hope which shows us how the Good Fridays of our life can result in an Easter Sunday. A resurrection to know there is nothing we cannot overcome.

# SHARING THE JOURNEY:

*Temporary hope is all around, but through my savior is PERMANENT hope that nothing can snatch away.*

*I now know Lord that by the power of your crucifixion you came back even stronger. You were now understood by those who followed you and proof of your overcoming death validated everything. I know that my own daily trails and life event crucifixions are no different. When I rise after being tormented, torn down, or seen as a failure, others have to look at me and see me as someone who believes at all costs and is fulfilled by you.*

# PRAYER:

*Jesus, redeemer of the world and conqueror of death, I receive your glorified presence in the Eucharist so I remain filled with the hope of every promise you have offered. Help me to know my setbacks are only temporary and in you I will find all I need to rise above to stumbling blocks in front of me.*

# Reflection

_____

_____

_____

_____

_____

_____

_____

_____

_____

_____

_____

_____

_____

_____

# WHO DO YOU SAY I AM?

---

*"Since Christ Himself has said, "This is My Body" who shall dare to doubt that It is His Body?" ~St. Cyril of Jerusalem*

---

Right now you are being asked the question, *"But who do you say that I am?"* (Mt 16:15) Throughout this book, I have offered snippets of Scripture to relate the story of salvation contained within the Eucharist. I have provided principles of the Catholic faith by referencing the Catechism of the Catholic Church for a deeper understanding of the doctrine we believe in; the precepts of our faith. I have given you my vision of what I believe Christ is saying to you from the moment you say, "Amen," you believe, till you head back to pray after you have consumed His body, blood, soul and divinity. Still, it has to come from you. The way you recognize Him, the manner in which you hold Him and how deeply you encounter Him within the depths of all you are. He once asked the disciples in this exchange recounted in the Gospel of Matthew

> *"... he asked his disciples, "Who do people say that the Son of Man is?" They replied, "Some say John the Baptist,\* others Elijah, still others Jeremiah or one of the prophets." 'But who do you say that I am?' Simon Peter said in reply, 'You are the Messiah, the Son of the living God.' Jesus said to him in reply, 'Blessed are you, Simon son of Jonah. For flesh and blood has not revealed this to you, but my heavenly Father.'"* (Mk 16:13-17)

Peter got the answer right. Jesus wasn't looking for the theological answer or the correct response others around them might be offering. He wanted to know where His disciples stood, so not only would they be ready to move beyond the point of His crucifixion, but that they would be able to share His church with the world long after He ascended to Heaven. However, did He just really want to know who the disciples thought He was as He stood in front of them? I believe He was asking something more than just that.

In my perception, He really wasn't looking for the words the disciples were going to offer. Actually, His question wasn't really to determine who they even thought Jesus might technically be. Instead, I believe His question actually could be interpreted as, "Who do you say you are?" The actions of the disciples determined whether they truly believe or not. In that moment they could say anything they would hope to please Christ in giving the "correct" answer. He wanted their response to hold conviction in the person of Christ so they were ready for what was yet to come.

In the same way, today, He is asking you the question, "Who do you say you are?" Do you walk up to receive me in the Eucharist knowing I love you unconditionally? "Do you even hold to the truth it is Me at all?" "How do your friends reflect the life you wish to live in relationship with me?" Just like the disciples, we have to answer these questions daily. Our answer to who we think Jesus is, is ultimately solidified by who we say we are as His children and Church in all we think, say and do.

We can say that finding Jesus in the Eucharist is never looking beyond our self. A transparent tabernacle we become which lets the world connect with Christ through us and because of us. Ultimately, we are working to become closer to the One who created us and that was Christ's job. Yes, it is His sacrifice which redeemed the world, but it was always about the Father in the end. The King will rule, but only in the Kingdom created by the Father. Likewise, it's never about us, but what we offer while glorifying Christ so we can spend eternity with Him. All through what was accomplished by the salvation history which we now know is contained within the Eucharist.

One of my favorite roles to contribute to while at my home parish is "Eucharistic Minister" or "Extraordinary Minister of Holy Communion" in its proper title; basically, the lay people who have the honor to distribute the body and blood of Christ at Communion. Part of the reason I love it so much (beside getting to hold Christ in my hands and share Him with others) is how people come up to receive Him in the Eucharist. I can tell just by the demeanor they stroll up the aisle. The way their eyes look at the host and even the words they choose to offer when they receive Communion, gives me a gut feeling whether or not they truly believe it's Christ present. I don't want to concentrate on the ones who don't, but instead revel in the beauty of those who know it's Him! Wide eyed, smiling, adoringly transfixed as they receive

Him and offer their "Amen" or quite even possibly letting a "Thank You" roll of their tongue. When that exchange happens, there is a connection between us as believers that makes the hair on my neck immediately stand up and tears come to my eyes. It's almost as if we are sharing a different language which is secret. Not because others aren't supposed to know, rather because we are willing to surrender to it. They take Him from my hands as if I just took His body from the cross, or out of the tomb and entrusting Him to their care. This is proof that the recognition of Christ's presence is not the same as openly experiencing the Real presence of God whole-heartedly. Those moments, for those people, the answer is clear when Christ is asking, "Who do you say that I am?"

Finding Jesus in the Eucharist is the growth we need to see more clearly with the eyes of the One we worship. Becoming the living vessel which makes Him visible for the entire world to see and experience. A chance for all to see what we see because we know what He gave us. Our opportunity to be the church in order to define our Savior through our joy, trust and works in a way which presents the resurrected Christ and not the crucified One; the glorified leader and not the despised trouble maker.

I pray you always know that there is no greater gift He could have ever given us than Himself. The words the Priest or Deacon prays as they pour the water into the wine during Communion preparation highlight this gift: *"May we come to share in the divinity of Christ who humbled himself to share in our humanity."* For us to share in His divinity means He has opened a gateway for us to take on all of Him to help us see the beauty of a life focused on His unconditional love. May each of us now use our humanity to bring divinity to this world through the faith we put on display, inspired by Jesus Christ found in the Eucharist. Let us journey with joy on our faces to tell the world, "Love wins."

It is our duty as Catholic Christians to appreciate the gift of the Eucharist for more than being just part of our Sunday obligation. It's our chance to find Him and all He wants for us through a relationship only He can give us through this Sacrament. God knows every desire within your heart, He is only asking you to consciously share it with Him so He can fill those places with all the wonderful attributes laid out before you in the Eucharist. Unconditionally, He comes to you and asks you come to Him the same way.

He is waiting for you; do not let another moment slip by without experiencing Him through the gift of the Eucharist. He is always present in your life but through your "Amen" He will become one with you.

> It is true. I stand at the door of your heart, day and night. Even when you are not listening, even when you doubt it could be Me, I am there. I await even the smallest sign of your response, even the least whispered invitation that will allow Me to enter.

> And I want you to know that whenever you invite Me, I do come always without fail. Silent and unseen I come, but with infinite power and love, and bringing the many gifts of My spirit. I come with My mercy, with My desire to forgive and heal you and with a love for you beyond your comprehension- a love every bit as great as the love I have received from the Father ( As much as the Father has loved me, I have loved you..."[John.15:9]). I come —

*longing to console you and give you strength, to lift you up and bind all your wounds. I bring you My light, to dispel your darkness and all your doubts. I come with My power, that I might carry you and all of your burdens; with My grace, to touch your heart and transform your life; and My peace I give to still your soul.*

*I know you through and through – I know everything about you. The very hairs of your head I have numbered. Nothing in your life is unimportant to Me. I have followed you through the years, and I have always loved you – even in your wanderings. I know everyone of your problems. I know your needs and your worries. And yes, I know all your sins. But I tell you again that I love you- not for what you have or haven't done – I love you for you, for the beauty and dignity My Father gave you by creating you in His own image. It is a dignity you have often forgotten, a beauty you have tarnished by sin. But I love you as you are, and I have shed My Blood to win you back. If you only ask Me with faith, My grace will touch all the needs changing in your life; and I will give you the strength to free yourself from sin and all its destructive power.*

*I know what is in your heart- I know your loneliness and all your hurts- the rejections, the judgments, the humiliations. I carried it all before you. And I carried it all for you, so you might share My strength and victory. I know especially your need for love – how you are thirsted in vain, by seeking that love selfishly, striving to fill the emptiness inside you with passing pleasures- with the even greater emptiness of sin. Do you thirst for love? "Come to Me all of you who thirst..."(John 7:37). I will satisfy you and fill you. Do you thirst to be cherished? I cherish you more than you can imagine – to the point of dying on a cross for you...*

*(Excerpt of the Meditation "I Thirst for You" based on the spiritual teachings of Mother Teresa of Calcutta)*

# UNCONDITIONALLY

# The Anima Christi

SOUL OF CHRIST, SANCTIFY ME
BODY OF CHRIST, SAVE ME
BLOOD OF CHRIST, INEBRIATE ME
WATER FROM THE SIDE OF CHRIST, WASH ME
PASSION OF CHRIST, STRENGTHEN ME
O GOOD JESUS, HEAR ME
WITHIN YOUR WOUNDS HIDE ME
SEPARATED FROM YOU LET ME NEVER BE
FROM THE EVIL ONE PROTECT ME
AT THE HOUR OF MY DEATH CALL ME
AND BID ME COME UNTO THEE
THAT I MAY PRAISE YOU WITH YOUR SAINTS
FOREVER AND EVER
AMEN

Part of praying specific prayers we are taught, or we find on our own, is to create a connection point to where we feel ourselves in an embrace with the Holy One. Especially when the words of our prayers allow us to see the beauty of our faith and experience God's presence. All of these moments when the words written on the page becoming a living moment of worship and petition should transform us in some way. They give us an opportunity to lift our hearts to the Lord even when we don't have the right words or we are too weak to even think straight. Finding Jesus in the Eucharist can be accomplished by opening up ourselves to make specific connections. Inviting Him to become part of our every moment.

> *Once committed to conversion, the heart learns to pray*
> *in faith. Faith is a filial adherence to God beyond what we*
> *feel and understand. It is possible because the beloved*
> *Son gives us access to the Father. He can ask us to "seek"*
> *and to "knock," since he himself is the door and the way.*
> *(CCC 2609)*

Of the many prayers that fall under the "Eucharist" category of prayer is the *Anima Christi*. Personally, I feel the deepest connection to Christ and all He offers me when I lift up its words. It's a beautiful collection of the various fruits of Jesus offered through receiving the Eucharist. Many years ago when looking through a Catholic prayer book, I came across this all-encompassing prayer. It showed me what it means to find the peace of Jesus within the Eucharist.

The Anima Christi has been attributed to a wide array of authors. Some believe as far back as the fifth century, but most scholars confer its usage at least dating back to the fourteenth century. A wider exposure came about when the prayer became part of St. Ignatius' spiritual exercises. Despite its historical origin, safe to say it's been around a long time. Outside of scripture, I find such beauty in the unification with all people of our faith to know we are offering the same prayers today that others lifted up hundreds of years prior.

Anima Christi is Latin for, "Soul of Christ." So we understand before we speak any other words of the prayer, we are reflecting on the enveloping heavenly soul of Christ and not merely the human body. The soul holds His will and is what returns to the Father. The prayer goes on to give us aspects of our baptism, the Lord's passion and even our own birth into a new life in the Kingdom of Heaven; all this contained in the sanctifying grace present in the soul of Christ. A soul that we are allowed to touch when we partake in the Feast of the Eucharist.

Let's call to mind the divine power within Christ's being by examining each verse. Praying together in thanksgiving for the opportunity to find Jesus' saving grace revealed in the Blessed Sacrament.

## SOUL OF CHRIST, SANCTIFY ME

There is no purer soul in the history of time than that of Jesus Christ. A soul that encountered temptation, compassion, love, anger and even fear. However, in all of His humanity, Jesus remained holy which not only kept Him pure of heart, but also pure of soul. In this line, we are asking for him to make us holy; sanctified. The word "sanctify" would be simply defined as: to set apart as or declare holy; consecrate. For us to be consecrated through the Eucharist helps us to settle into a realm of covenant with God which commences when we are separate from ourselves and invite Christ into us to become one with Him. *"See, I am now establishing my covenant with you and your descendants after you and with every living creature that was with you: the birds, the tame animals, and all the wild animals that were with you—all that came out of the ark."* (Gen 9:9-10)

Noah, Aaron and Moses all had a chance to die to themselves and be made whole in Him. In the same way, we are desiring holiness, freedom from sin and whatever else may bind us. We look to be relieved from anything which does not allow us to fully encounter Jesus both inside and outside of the Eucharist. As the Catechism identifies for us in relation to his dissension into hell we proclaim in our creed:

> *"In his human soul united to his divine person, the dead Christ went down to the realm of the dead. He opened heaven's gates for the just who had gone before him."* (CCC 637)

This is important to recognize for us in the moments after receiving Him in the Eucharist because this is what we desire in being relieved from our brokenness. In some cases, to close the distance we have placed before us and Christ.

We begin the prayer to say, "Lord make me holy as You were holy in both your humanness and divinity to join together with our soul in order to help us separate the things of this world preparing us for our true home in Heaven."

## BODY OF CHRIST, SAVE ME

Our goal as Catholic Christians is to live a life centered on faith so we might spend eternity with the One who created us. He gave us the gift of His Son who sacrificed His body for us so we could be saved. The words Christ spoke to the disciples gives us full understanding of how to live forever with him in Paradise: *"I am the living bread that came down from heaven; whoever eats this bread will live forever; and the bread that I will give is my flesh for the life of the world."* (Jn 6:51) By partaking in His body during Holy Communion we are connecting ourselves unconditionally with His promise. There was nothing else that He could give us as a human being which could have showed us not only the love He has for us, but how far He was willing to go in order to save us. This is our invitation to be saved. Christ's human body was sacrificed so He could defeat death and save us from the sins we commit.

Our prayer in this moment turns attention through the actual way He saved us on the cross. "Jesus may the body you once walked this Earth, which you offered back to the Father for me on the cross, be fulfilled in me. I know you gave it all for me that I may have the strength to give it all for you. Save me from my own human desires."

## BLOOD OF CHRIST, INEBRIATE ME

There is something special which comes with the request in this line of the prayer. We are not coming up to receive the blood of Christ in order to just get a chance to drink wine in church. It's Christ's most precious blood present which has a chance to pour into all the places we have not allowed Him into in our lives. (Note: We receive both the body and blood of Christ whether we receive only bread, only wine or both; He is fully present under both "species."-forms of the Eucharist).

The word inebriate literally means to be "drunk." Wait a second, are we asking Jesus to make us intoxicated with His blood? Yes... well in a way, but not the way we normally think of it. We are asking to be consumed in His blood which produces a euphoric glimpse of the love He has for us. So drunk physically? No. Drunk with love? Yes! Webster's Dictionary would use an alternate phrase: "to exhilarate."

By praying this we are removing ourselves from the physical aspects and related properties of the wine in the chalice and inviting God to make His love so powerfully evident through His blood, it produces a feeling which transforms us through the sensations only a real relationship with the Lord can provide.

Here, we meditate to say, "Lord allow this drink of your blood to place me into a one-on-one relationship with you. An intimacy nothing else on Earth can give me. May I be made whole once again to share in the amazing jubilation of ecstasy which only You can provide."

## WATER FROM THE SIDE OF CHRIST, WASH ME

What initially comes to mind is the moment when the soldier plunges his lance into the side of Jesus on the cross. No more blood remains, only water pours out. Church teaching would tell us the Holy Spirit sprang forth in that moment as the living water. Regardless, I would wish to be showered at the foot of the cross by anything Christ had left to pour out of Himself for me. Especially if it would cleanse me from the offenses which put Him there in the first place. Since we now know we are sacramentally forgiven of sin through water in Baptism, then this is a moment to seek the same reconciliation through Christ bound in the Eucharist.

*"The blood and water that flowed from the pierced side of the crucified Jesus are types of Baptism and the Eucharist, the sacraments of new life. From then on, it is possible 'to*

*be born of water and the Spirit' in order to enter the King-dom of God." (CCC 1225)*

This is the connection to the forgiveness of venial offenses wiped out through the Eucharist.

We ask now, "Lord, shower me in the waters of your grace. Make me clean of all the times I have sinned and strayed from you."

## PASSION OF CHRIST, STRENGTHEN ME

The journey involved in the Passion gives us the ability to connect ourselves with the strength is took for Jesus to get from the Last Supper to the cross. After all, He wasn't just seized and killed in the streets immediately. Christ not only knew what would happen as (evident in the tears he shed in the garden) but He needed to find inner strength to accept the Father's will. Where does the strength come from which would allow Him to complete what He came to do despite his fear? The answer is He loved us that much, a way we should be strong enough to love him back.

He died His human death for you and I. Think about what He endured for us, how strong He must have been when all seemed lost. We are striving to share in this courage and strength to remain vigilant for the road we travel on. Knowing that our Good Friday might be what we are experiencing, now, while understanding it yields our own personal, Easter Sunday triumph.

Through His Passion we plead, "Lord please give me the

grace I need to be strong enough just as you were to fulfill your ultimate purpose. Allow me to remember how your obedience changed the world and that in your image I will have the resolve to get through anything. When I fall help me get up and keep going."

## O GOOD JESUS, HEAR ME

Our Lord likes us to plead our case sometimes. Since this is a prayer request it's okay to let Him know how much it means by really asking for His attention. After all, He gave us a model of prayer to not only spend time in quiet prayer, but our scriptures tell us He was also willing to converse directly with the Father for what He needed. Our initial desire to pray during the Eucharist should be in Thanksgiving for the gift of the sacrifice we are about to, or have, received. However, when we feel a connection to Christ there is a moment where we desire a chance for Him to hear what has fallen on our heart to request in that specific moment.

> "...Jesus hears the prayer of faith, expressed in words (the leper, Jairus, the Canaanite woman, the good thief) or in silence (the bearers of the paralytic, the woman with a hemorrhage who touches his clothes, the tears and ointment of the sinful woman). The urgent request of the blind men, "Have mercy on us, Son of David" or "Jesus, Son of David, have mercy on me!" has-been renewed in the traditional prayer to Jesus known as the Jesus Prayer: "Lord Jesus Christ, Son of God, have mercy on me, a sinner!" Healing infirmities or forgiving sins, Jesus always responds to a prayer offered in faith: "Your faith has made you well; go in peace." (CCC 2616)

Confidently we pray, "Jesus I know you hear my words, but take note to what my heart cries out for that I cannot verbalize. I come to you, pleading with humility to not only receive my prayers but to answer them as you see fit."

## WITHIN YOUR WOUNDS HIDE ME SEPARATED FROM YOU LET ME NEVER BE

When Thomas doubted that Christ had actually risen from the dead, the only thing which would make him believe would be to place his fingers inside his wounds (Jn 20:25). Scripture never tells us that Thomas actually did it, but even as hard as the wounds are to accept during the crucifixion, they are equally as comforting after the resurrection. We can assume the wounds of Christ he saw reassured him it truly was the Lord in his midst.

For each of us, there is safety of sitting deep inside the nail holes and lance wound which make us feel surrounded, immersed in Christ's protection. If we are this close with the risen Lord in the Eucharist, we cease to exist on our own. A safe place within Christ knowing nothing can harm us because our Savior overcame death and conquered it so we may have eternal life. *"But he was pierced for our sins, crushed for our iniquity. He bore the punishment that makes us whole, by his wounds we were healed."* (Is 53:5) We will be doubters from time to time but even when we have separated ourselves from Christ, we will remain bound in Him through His wounds. Not by sight, but by faith.

When we allow ourselves to experience this peace and fully find Jesus in the Eucharist by accepting his Real Presence in consuming Him (just as Thomas did in seeing Him), we never want to be separated from Him. It's almost to say the Shepherd no longer uses a staff to guide us, but we are one with Him, walking confidently because we live in Him and He lives in us.

For safety and comfort, we ask, "Jesus without you I would have nothing and I would be nothing. In my own questions of faith and even fears, stay by my side and remind me of your presence. Wrap me in your love and let me never feel alone despite my moments of doubt."

## FROM THE EVIL ONE PROTECT ME

As I talked about in the chapter "Temptation in the Desert," spiritual warfare is real. We have a tendency to avoid the conversation about the threat of spiritual warfare. It's a subject which can seem too intense to accept to exist or one we are just not comfortable admitting. With that said, it is part of everyday living.

When we allow ourselves to surrender to God's plan, there is a major threat to the evil one's efforts to persuade us into sin. Whether they come in the form of simple distractions or blatant, vicious confrontations persuaded by the devil, they can and will occur.

This portion of the prayer is vital for our ultimate defense to recognize and thwart evil's attempts to send us spiraling into doubt, question what we believe or commit acts of sin. We already offer a similar request when we pray the Our Father in the line, "Lead us not into temptation but deliver us from evil." God would never directly lead us to offend Him. We are just begging to not have to endure the test which our humanness is not always strong enough to make the right moral and virtuous decisions.

Since evil is the absence of good, it's not even for defense against the acts which we could tempted to commit but additionally the apathy to slip away from faithfulness. We've already learned how through inaction we are seduced into disobedience. We are praying to recognize the presence which causes all this to happen by relying on the image of Christ tempted in the desert and the garden. A powerful image Paul gave to the Ephesians:

> "Finally, draw your strength from the Lord and from his mighty power. Put on the armor of God so that you may be able to stand firm against the tactics of the devil. For our struggle is not with flesh and blood but with the principalities, with the powers, with the world rulers of this present darkness, with the evil spirits in the heavens. Therefore, put on the armor of God, that you may be able to resist on the evil day and, having done everything, to hold your ground." (Eph (6:10-13)

Let us not be so naïve to think that same Prince of Darkness who got Adam and Eve banished from paradise, made Job suffer to prove his faithfulness and had the gull to attempt to persuade Jesus away from His Father, wouldn't come after us. Especially when we long to live a Christ centered life, striving to spend eternity in Heaven.

This verse is a reiteration of the protection the wounds of Christ grant us when we are hidden with them, "Lord, I beg you to keep the devil far from me. I am not always strong enough to ignore his temptations, nor continuously making the right decisions which would keep me from offending You. Remain my protector against every advance of Satan."

## AT THE HOUR OF MY DEATH CALL ME AND BID ME COME UNTO THEE

When our time is up, will we feel worthy of His love? Anything but a resounding "yes" could make us feel distance in those final hours. The power of this line is its appeal to not be alone as our soul prepares for eternal rest. A final moment of peace, understanding and clarity that Jesus is with us. We have nothing to fear during the final moments of our Earthly life if we live a Christ centered life. United with our Lord through His dying and resurrection we receive a final Holy Communion. One last feast with the Lord as He prepares all we are for our road to Heaven.

> *"The Christian who unites his own death to that of Jesus views it as a step towards him and an entrance into everlasting life. When the Church for the last time speaks Christ's words of pardon and absolution over the dying Christian, seals him for the last time with a strengthening anointing, and gives him Christ in viaticum (A final Holy Communion) as nourishment for the journey" (CCC 1020)*

We are making it known to God by praying this line that we desire to spend our days with Him. A declaration we crave for Him to be with us so we might be with Him. We find comfort in the words spoken by Jesus in John's Gospel when he promised, *"My sheep hear my voice; I know them, and they follow me. I give them eternal life, and they shall never perish. No one can take them out of my hand. My Father, who has given them to me, is greater than all, and no one can take them out of the Father's hand."* (Jn 10:27-29)

So likewise we pray, "Lord be with me in my final moments so that you will call me home. Holding my hand to provide me with all I need to make a peaceful journey to enter into your Kingdom."

## THAT I MAY PRAISE YOU WITH YOUR SAINTS, FOREVER AND EVER

How could we ever repay God for all He has done for us other than to praise Him at His throne along with all those who have gone before us? Gaining Heaven isn't just about avoiding hell or a place where God is not evident. It's about the opportunity to rejoice in the eternal banquet which is filled with all those who have gone before us in the communion of saints.

If we have praised Him on Earth in all things in the appropriate manner and time, I imagine Heaven will not be any different; it's our home. We were made by God to return to God. Or as St. Anselm of Canterbury plainly puts it, "No one will have any other desire in heaven than what God wills; and the desire of one will be the desire of all; and the desire of all and of each one will also be the desire of God."

In that image we offer the closing of this prayer, "Lord there will be no greater glory than to be with you forever and ever as our entire community of believers joins together with love to glorify you each day. You made me to return to you and through the Eucharist I experienced the Heaven where you dwell and seek to be there always."

Now that I have shared my reflection on the beauty of the Anima Christi, I would like to offer you another insight to my own personal prayer which came about as an extension of the words we just examined. I have taken the precepts of the Anima Christi and let it become the foundation of not only my "after communion" reflection, but also my personal preparation during the consecration of the bread. As each gift ("Species" to be theologically correct) is lifted in the form as to which our eyes can process, I pray these words:

### As the bread is elevated:

*Lord Jesus, I am humbled that you have presented your-self to me in this gift of the Eucharist. I pray that I will be nourished physically and spiritually through your Bread of Life. Allow your bones to become my strength and your flesh to envelope me in your grace. I desire to become one with you so I may hunger no more as I journey to-ward your Kingdom.*

### As Chalice is raised:

*Jesus thank you for the gift of your sacrifice and your blood poured out for me, now present before me. When I drink from this cup, allow your blood to flow into my veins making me one with you so nothing will ever sepa-rate us. Allow me to become consubstantial with you so I might have the courage and strength to be your hands, feet and eyes for the world because You live in me. May the waters from your side wash me when I have failed you and let me thirst no more for your love. May I never forget the sacrifice you offered for me on that Good Fri-day.*

Feel free to adapt this prayer or any prayer which allows you to fully connect with Christ in the Eucharist. I invite you to even write your own. Revise the wording so it speaks from your heart in the way which you speak so the words are not uncomfortable to repeat. Create a time and space where you are talking with God, giving homage to the Savior who gave His life for us. Let it free you from the distractions of life and help you to become transformed through the grace in which only the Bread of Life can offer; unconditionally connected to Jesus Christ found crucified and resurrected in the Eucharist.

# Adoration

*"Our Lord does not come down from heaven every day to lie in a golden ciborium. He comes to find another heaven which is infinitely dearer to him—the heaven of our souls, created in his image, the living temples of the adorable Trinity."*
~ *St. Therese of Lisieux*

Not every church offers Eucharistic Adoration formally while some have twenty-four hour chapels dedicated to this devotion. No matter where you experience Adoration, something beautiful happens in silence that calls us to refocus on what we believe. Honestly assessing how we are living what we proclaim to believe. This is the kind of inner peace that occurs when we are still and have placed ourselves before the Blessed Sacrament. Could it be as good as literally being present with Christ? Like John at the Last Supper? *"One of his disciples, the one whom Jesus loved, was reclining at Jesus' side."* (Jn 13:23) What it must have been like to lay at Christ's side or even the moment *"He leaned back against Jesus' chest..."* (Jn 13:25) to ask his Lord a question. The wonderful opportunity of Eucharistic Adoration gives us the same chance. To sit with Jesus Christ, present before us, without worry, expectation or wonder.

Saint Pope John Paul II said this of Eucharistic Adoration in his encyclical *Ecclesia de Eucharistia*

> *"The worship of the Eucharist outside of the Mass is of inestimable value for the life of the Church… It is pleasant to spend time with him, to lie close to his breast like the Beloved Disciple (cf. Jn 13:25) and to feel the infinite love present in his heart. If in our time Christians must be distinguished above all by the "art of prayer", how can we not feel a renewed need to spend time…in silent adoration, in heartfelt love before Christ present in the Most Holy Sacrament? How often, dear brothers and sisters, have I experienced this, and drawn from it strength, consolation and support!…Saint Alphonsus Liguori…wrote: "Of all devotions, that of adoring Jesus in the Blessed Sacrament is the greatest after the sacraments, the one dearest to God and the one most helpful to us." The Eucharist is a priceless treasure: by not only celebrating it but also by praying before it outside of Mass we are enabled to make contact with the very wellspring of grace… In the course of the day the faithful should not omit visiting the Blessed Sacrament…" ~Pope John Paull !!*

The first question people often ask is, "What am I supposed to do in Adoration?" I can't think of a better answer than the one laid out in Psalm 46:11, *"Be still and know that I am God."* It is our willingness to acknowledge what we believe in the Eucharist which leads us to take the time to be with Jesus. The Catechism gives us the understanding of what Adoration means for us as Catholic Christians:

> *Adoration is the first attitude of man acknowledging that he is a creature before his Creator. It exalts the greatness of the Lord who made us and the almighty power of the Savior who sets us free from evil. Adoration is homage of the spirit to the "King of Glory," respectful silence in the presence of the "ever greater" God. (CCC 2628)*

So while we don't have to "do" anything specific, we should try to become one with Him by utilizing our time not only to talk, but to connect through Sacred Scripture, books and prayers which help us grow in our faith along with our personal relationship with Christ. Some people pray the rosary, while some simply gaze at the offering of unconditional love before them. While others might journal about what they are hearing in prayer.

Once we have removed the expectation of having to do "something" in Adoration, then the follow up usually is, "Well what is it anyway?" The United States Conference of Catholic Bishops give us this definition to put this worship opportunity into perspective:

> "This (Exposition and Benediction) is an extension of the adoration of the Blessed Sacrament which occurs in every Mass: 'Behold the Lamb of God, behold him who takes away the sins of the world. Blessed are those called to the supper of the Lamb.' Exposition of the Blessed Sacrament flows from the sacrifice of the Mass and serves to deepen our hunger for Communion with Christ and the rest of the Church."

This is our moment to fall more deeply in love with Christ, while not having to remember to sit, stand or kneel, but simply be with Him. Finding Jesus in the Eucharist goes beyond receiving Him physically, but it's his offering of unconditional love found in spiritual communion as well.

When we desire to be with someone we love, the opportunity the share an embrace, or some sign of physical encounter that reaffirms our feelings. But we don't only feel love from that point forward only when we touch. We take time to rekindle our emotions through other forms of interacting, from writing letters to texting, talking on the telephone or even a wave from across the room when you can't seem to reach each other. We find ways to share a moment of connectivity and love.

Adoration gives us similar moments to spend time with our Bridegroom, with a connection of conversation, prayer and praise. A follow up question might then be to ask, "Why do I have to have Jesus in the Sacrament present to pray to Him or talk with Him?" Answer is, "You don't." However, when we take advantage of His real presence before us, our human senses are once again enabling us to experience everything differently.

When you commit to spending time with Christ in Adoration, make a point to journal about your time together. Take into account all you hear and experience. We wouldn't have to Bible without the authors who weren't willing to record the word's the Holy Spirit was sending to them. By writing down our thoughts we can connect the thoughts to where we were once in our life and what Jesus wanted us to know in response to either our trials or victories. When we document our encounters, they might be the thing we refer back to when we feel distance come between us and God.

Lastly, expect the unexpected. Don't talk yourself out of the beauty of what you experienced. Don't be fooled to think the opportunity we are given by God to spend time with Him in Adoration has to be about what we can get out of it; we unite with other believers who are the body of Christ. all part of the beauty of spending time with Him to simply adore Him. Not to seek grace but to soak it in. Not to expect anything, but to give everything.

I have found that one of the things which keeps many people from participating in certain events within the church or be part of some traditions, is not knowing what it's all about. Then even if they decide to commit, a lack of knowledge of terminology, what's happening, when or why certain rituals are performed, make them feel like an outsider. Since I want you to experience the beauty of our Lord in the Eucharist in every way possible, I wanted to give you just a few terms which will ease your anxiety. Worst case, look around your own parish and say, "Ohhhh, now I know what that is."

So, from the Catholic Chronicles of *"Why do we do that? And What is that?"* (not a real set of books, I just made it up), here are some terms you may or may not be familiar with which relate to the Eucharist, Holy Hour and specifically, Eucharistic Adoration:

**Host**: A victim of sacrifice, and therefore the consecrated Bread of the Eucharist considered as the sacrifice of the Body of Christ. The word is also used of the round wafers used for consecration. (Etym. Latin hostia, sacrificial offering.)

**Ciborium:** A covered container used to hold the consecrated small Hosts. It is similar to a chalice but covered and larger, used for small Communion hosts of the faithful.

**Tabernacle:** A cupboard or boxlike receptacle for the exclusive reservation of the Blessed Sacrament. In early Christian times the sacred species was reserved in the home because of possible persecution. Later dove-shaped tabernacles were suspended by chains before the altar. Nowadays tabernacles may be round or rectangular and made of wood, stone, or metal. They are covered with a veil and lined with precious metal or silk, with a corporal beneath the ciboria or other sacred vessels.

**Sanctuary Lamp**: A wax candle, generally in a red glass container, kept burning day and night wherever the Blessed Sacrament is reserved in Catholic churches or chapels. It is an emblem of Christ's abiding love and a reminder to the faithful to respond with loving adoration in return.

**Monstrance**: (From Latin monstrare: to show) The sacred vessel (also called "ostensorium") used for the exposition and adoration of the Blessed Sacrament as well as solemn Benediction. The general form and shape of the monstrance is a round glass or crystal-covered opening through which the Sacred Host can be seen. The glass enclosure is frequently surrounded by rays or other decorations. These indicate the graces and spiritual blessings that flow from the Holy Eucharist upon those who adore and worship It. The glass enclosure, or "luna," is held up by a stem or base, allowing the monstrance to be placed on an altar or carried in procession.

**Humeral Veil:** A long oblong piece of silk or vestment material often richly ornamented or embroidered, worn over the shoulders and covering the hands of the priest as he gives the blessing with the Sacred Host in the monstrance at benediction.

**Exposition:** The ceremony in which a priest or deacon removes the Sacred Host from the tabernacle and places it on the altar for adoration. In public exposition the Sacred Host is placed in the lunette of the monstrance and elevated so that all adorers can see it. In private expositions the tabernacle door is opened and the ciborium containing consecrated Hosts is brought forward. Some churches, religious monasteries and convents with special permission have the Sacred Host perpetually exposed for special honor and devotion with someone in attendance night and day.

**Down in Adoration Falling:** (Tantum ergo Sacramentum), this hymn pays homage to our Lord both in the Eucharist and in His glory in the Trinity

*This great Sacrament we hail;*

*Over ancient forms of worship*

*Newer rites of grace prevail;*

*Faith will tell us Christ is present,*

*When our human senses fail.*

*To the everlasting Father,*

*And the Son who made us free,*

*And the Spirit, God proceeding*

*From them Each eternally,*

*Be salvation, honor, blessing,*

*Might and endless majesty. Amen.*

**Benediction:** is a rite in which a priest or deacon pronounces a blessing over those who are present for Eucharistic adoration. As he gives the blessing, he elevates the monstrance or other vessel that contains the sacred host. Benediction normally follows a period of prayer before the Blessed Sacrament, just prior to its reposition into the Tabernacle.

**Divine Praises:** A series of praises, recited for generations after the benediction of the Blessed Sacrament. They are thought to have been originally compiled in 1797 in reparation for blasphemy and profane language. Praise of the Immaculate Conception, her bodily Assumption into heaven, the Sacred Heart, St. Joseph, and the Precious Blood have been added since the middle of the nineteenth century. The present text reads:

*Blessed be God.*

*Blessed be his holy Name.*

*Blessed be Jesus Christ, true God and true man.*

*Blessed be the name of Jesus.*

*Blessed be his most Sacred Heart.*

*Blessed be his most Precious Blood.*

*Blessed be Jesus in the most holy*
*Sacrament of the Altar.*

*Blessed be the Holy Spirit, the Paraclete.*

*Blessed be the great Mother of God, Mary most holy.*

*Blessed be her holy and Immaculate Conception.*

*Blessed be her glorious Assumption.*

*Blessed be the name of Mary, Virgin and Mother.*

*Blessed be St. Joseph, her most chaste spouse.*

*Blessed be God in his angels and in his saints.*

**Reposition:** When the priest or deacon has blessed everyone he then replaces the Blessed Sacrament in the tabernacle and genuflects. The following acclamation may be said at this time. This acclamation is called the Divine Praises.

*Holy God, we praise thy name;*
*Lord of all, we bow before thee;*
*All on earth they scepter claim;*
*All in heaven above adore thee.*
*Infinite they vast domain,*
*Everlasting is thy reign!*

# Catechism References

# Chapter I Reference
## The Desire for God

**27** The desire for God is written in the human heart, because man is created by God and for God; and God never ceases to draw man to himself. Only in God will he find the truth and happiness he never stops searching for:

> The dignity of man rests above all on the fact that he is called to communion with God. This invitation to converse with God is addressed to man as soon as he comes into being. For if man exists it is because God has created him through love, and through love continues to hold him in existence. He cannot live fully according to truth unless he freely acknowledges that love and entrusts himself to his creator.[1]

**28** In many ways, throughout history down to the present day, men have given expression to their quest for God in their religious beliefs and behavior: in their prayers, sacrifices, rituals, meditations, and so forth. These forms of religious expression, despite the ambiguities they often bring with them, are so universal that one may well call man a religious being:

From one ancestor [God] made all nations to inhabit the whole earth, and he allotted the times of their existence and the boundaries of the places where they would live, so that they would search for God and perhaps grope for him and find him - though indeed he is not far from each one of us. For "in him we live and move and have our being."[2]

**29** But this "intimate and vital bond of man to God" (GS 19 § 1) can be forgotten, overlooked, or even explicitly rejected by man.[3] Such attitudes can have different causes: revolt against evil in the world; religious ignorance or indifference; the cares and riches of this world; the scandal of bad example on the part of believers; currents of thought hostile to religion; finally, that attitude of sinful man which makes him hide from God out of fear and flee his call.[4]

**30** "Let the hearts of those who seek the LORD rejoice."[5] Although man can forget God or reject him, He never ceases to call every man to seek him, so as to find life and happiness. But this search for God demands of man every effort of intellect, a sound will, "an upright heart", as well as the witness of others who teach him to seek God.

> You are great, O Lord, and greatly to be praised: great is your power and your wisdom is without measure. And man, so small a part of your creation, wants to praise you: this man, though clothed with mortality and bearing the evidence of sin and the proof that you withstand the proud. Despite everything, man, though but a small a part of your creation, wants to praise you. You yourself encourage him to delight in your praise, for you have made us for yourself, and our heart is restless until it rests in you.[6]

**44** Man is by nature and vocation a religious being. Coming from God, going toward God, man lives a fully human life only if he freely lives by his bond with God.

**45** Man is made to live in communion with God in whom he finds happiness: When I am completely united to you, there will be no more sorrow or trials; entirely full of you, my life will be complete (St. Augustine, Conf. 10, 28, 39: PL 32, 795}.

**1700** The dignity of the human person is rooted in his creation in the image and likeness of God (article 1); it is fulfilled in his vocation to divine beatitude (article 2). It is essential to a human being freely to direct himself to this fulfillment (article 3). By his deliberate actions (article 4), the human person does, or does not, conform to the good promised by God and attested by moral conscience (article 5). Human beings make their own contribution to their interior growth; they make their whole sentient and spiritual lives into means of this growth (article 6). With the help of grace they grow in virtue (article 7), avoid sin, and if they sin they entrust themselves as did the prodigal son[7] to the mercy of our Father in heaven (article 8). In this way they attain to the perfection of charity.

**1817** Hope is the theological virtue by which we desire the kingdom of heaven and eternal life as our happiness, placing our trust in Christ's promises and relying not on our own strength, but on the help of the grace of the Holy Spirit. "Let us hold fast the confession of our hope without wavering, for he who promised is faithful."[84] "The Holy Spirit . . . he poured out upon us richly through Jesus Christ our Savior, so that we might be justified by his grace and become heirs in hope of eternal life."[85]

1 Vatican Council II, GS 19 § 1.
2 Acts 17:26-28.
3 GS 19 § 1.
4 Cf. GS 19-21; Mt 13:22; Gen 3:8-10; Jon 1:3.
5 Ps 105:3.
6 St. Augustine, Conf. 1,1,1:PL 32,659-661.
7 Lk:15:11-32
84 *Heb* 10:23.
85 *Titus* 3:6-7.

# CHAPTER II REFERENCE
## WORTHINESS & FAITHFULNESS

**1386** Before so great a sacrament, the faithful can only echo humbly and with ardent faith the words of the Centurion: "Domine, non sum dignus ut intres sub tectum meum, sed tantum dic verbo, et sanabitur anima mea" ("Lord, I am not worthy that you should enter under my roof, but only say the word and my soul will be healed.").[219] And in the Divine Liturgy of St. John Chrysostom the faithful pray in the same spirit: O Son of God, bring me into communion today with your mystical supper. I shall not tell your enemies the secret, nor kiss you with Judas' kiss. But like the good thief I cry, "Jesus, remember me when you come into your kingdom."

**1388** It is in keeping with the very meaning of the Eucharist that the faithful, if they have the required dispositions,[221] receive communion when they participate in the Mass.[222] As the Second Vatican Council says: "That more perfect form of participation in the Mass whereby the faithful, after the priest's communion, receive the Lord's Body from the same sacrifice, is warmly recommended."[223]

**1817** Hope is the theological virtue by which we desire the kingdom of heaven and eternal life as our happiness, placing our trust in Christ's promises and relying not on our own strength, but on the help of the grace of the Holy Spirit. "Let us hold fast the confession of our hope without wavering, for he who promised is faithful."[84] "The Holy Spirit . . . he poured out upon us richly through Jesus Christ our Savior, so that we might be justified by his grace and become heirs in hope of eternal life."[85]

**2610** Just as Jesus prays to the Father and gives thanks before receiving his gifts, so he teaches us filial boldness: "Whatever you ask in prayer, believe that you receive it, and you will."[66] Such is the power of prayer and of faith that does not doubt: "all things are possible to him who believes."[67] Jesus is as saddened by the "lack of faith" of his own neighbors and the "little faith" of his own disciples[68] as he is struck with admiration at the great faith of the Roman centurion and the Canaanite woman.

219 Roman Missal, response to the invitation to communion; cf. Mt 8:8.
221 Cf. CIC, can. 916.
222 Cf. CIC, can. 917; The faithful may recieve the Holy Eucharist only a second time on the same day [CF. Pontificia Commissio Codici Iuris Canonici Authentice Intrepretando, Responsa ad proposita dubia, 1:AAS 76 (1984) 746]
223 SC 55.
84 Heb 10:23
85 Titus 3:6-7.
66 Mk 11:24.
67 Mk 9:23; cf. Mt 21:22.
68 Cf. Mk 6:6; Mt 8:26.
69 Cf. Mt 8:10;15:28.

# CHAPTER III REFERENCE
## TRINITY & UNION WITH CHRIST

**1331** *Holy Communion,* because by this sacrament we unite ourselves to Christ, who makes us sharers in his Body and Blood to form a single body.[151] We also call it: *the holy things (ta hagia; sancta)*[152] - the first meaning of the phrase "communion of saints" in the Apostles' Creed - *the bread of angels, bread from heaven, medicine of immortality,*[153] *viaticum.* . . .

**1370** To the offering of Christ are united not only the members still here on earth, but also those already *in the glory of heaven.* In communion with and commemorating the Blessed Virgin Mary and all the saints, the Church offers the Eucharistic sacrifice. In the Eucharist the Church is as it were at the foot of the cross with Mary, united with the offering and intercession of Christ.

**1391** *Holy Communion augments our union with Christ.* The principal fruit of receiving the Eucharist in Holy Communion is an intimate union with Christ Jesus. Indeed, the Lord said: "He who eats my flesh and drinks my blood abides in me, and I in him."[226] Life in Christ has its foundation in the Eucharistic banquet: "As the living Father sent me, and I live because of the Father, so he who eats me will live because of me."[227]

**1396** *The unity of the Mystical Body: the Eucharist makes the Church.* Those who receive the Eucharist are united more closely to Christ. Through it Christ unites them to all the faithful in one body - the Church. Communion renews, strengthens, and deepens this incorporation into the Church, already achieved by Baptism. In Baptism we have been called to form but one body.[233] The Eucharist fulfills this call: "The cup of blessing which we bless, is it not a participation in the blood of Christ? The bread which we break, is it not a participation in the body of Christ? Because there is one bread, we who are many are one body, for we all partake of the one bread:"[234]

If you are the body and members of Christ, then it is your sacrament that is placed on the table of the Lord; it is your sacrament that you receive. To that which you are you respond "Amen" ("yes, it is true!") and by responding to it you assent to it. For you hear the words, "the Body of Christ" and respond "Amen." Be then a member of the Body of Christ that your *Amen* may be true.[235]

**1419** Having passed from this world to the Father, Christ gives us in the Eucharist the pledge of glory with him. Participation in the Holy Sacrifice identifies us with his Heart, sustains our strength along the pilgrimage of this life, makes us long for eternal life, and unites us even now to the Church in heaven, the Blessed Virgin Mary, and all the saints.

151 Cf. 1 Cor 1016-17.
152 Apostolic Constitutions 8,13,12:PG 1,1108; Didache 9,5; 10:6:SCh 248,176-178.
226 Jn 6:56.
227 Jn 6:57.
228 Fanqith, Syriac Office of Antioch, Vol. I, Commun., 237a-b.
233 Cf. 1 Cor 12:13.
234 1 Cor 10:16-17.
235 St. Augustine, Sermo 272:PL 38,1247.

# CHAPTER IV REFERENCE
## MARY OUR MOTHER

**963** Since the Virgin Mary's role in the mystery of Christ and the Spirit has been treated, it is fitting now to consider her place in the mystery of the Church. "The Virgin Mary . . . is acknowledged and honored as being truly the Mother of God and of the redeemer. . . . She is 'clearly the mother of the members of Christ' . . . since she has by her charity joined in bringing about the birth of believers in the Church, who are members of its head."[502] "Mary, Mother of Christ, Mother of the Church."[503]

**964** Mary's role in the Church is inseparable from her union with Christ and flows directly from it. "This union of the mother with the Son in the work of salvation is made manifest from the time of Christ's virginal conception up to his death";[504] it is made manifest above all at the hour of his Passion:

> Thus the Blessed Virgin advanced in her pilgrimage of faith, and faithfully persevered in her union with her Son unto the cross. There she stood, in keeping with the divine plan, enduring with her only begotten Son the intensity of his suffering, joining herself with his sacrifice in her mother's heart, and lovingly consenting to the immolation of this victim, born of her: to be given, by the same Christ Jesus dying on the cross, as a mother to his disciple, with these words: "Woman, behold your son."[505]

**968** Her role in relation to the Church and to all humanity goes still further. "In a wholly singular way she cooperated by her obedience, faith, hope, and burning charity in the Savior's work of restoring supernatural life to souls. For this reason she is a mother to us in the order of grace."[511]

**971** "*All generations will call me blessed*": "The Church's devotion to the Blessed Virgin is intrinsic to Christian worship."[515] The Church rightly honors "the Blessed Virgin with special devotion. From the most ancient times the Blessed Virgin has been honored with the title of 'Mother of God,' to whose protection the faithful fly in all their dangers and needs. . . . This very special devotion . . . differs essentially from the adoration which is given to the incarnate Word and equally to the Father and the Holy Spirit, and greatly fosters this adoration."[516] The liturgical feasts dedicated to the Mother of God and Marian prayer, such as the rosary, an "epitome of the whole Gospel," express this devotion to the Virgin Mary.[517]

**973** By pronouncing her "fiat" at the Annunciation and giving her consent to the Incarnation, Mary was already collaborating with the whole work her Son was to accomplish. She is mother wherever he is Savior and head of the Mystical Body.

**975** "We believe that the Holy Mother of God, the new Eve, Mother of the Church, continues in heaven to exercise her maternal role on behalf of the members of Christ" (Paul VI, *CPG* § 15).'

**495** Called in the Gospels "the mother of Jesus", Mary is acclaimed by Elizabeth, at the prompting of the Spirit and even before the birth of her son, as "the mother of my Lord".[144] In fact, the One whom she conceived as man by the Holy Spirit, who truly became her Son according to the flesh, was none other than the Father's eternal Son, the second person of the Holy Trinity. Hence the Church confesses that Mary is truly "Mother of God" (Theotokos).[145]

**501** Jesus is Mary's only son, but her spiritual motherhood extends to all men whom indeed he came to save: "The Son whom she brought forth is he whom God placed as the first-born among many brethren, that is, the faithful in whose generation and formation she co-operates with a mother's love."[160]

**508** From among the descendants of Eve, God chose the Virgin Mary to be the mother of his Son. "Full of grace", Mary is "the most excellent fruit of redemption" (SC 103): from the first instant of her conception, she was totally preserved from the stain of original sin and she remained pure from all personal sin throughout her life.

**509** Mary is truly "Mother of God" since she is the mother of the eternal Son of God made man, who is God himself.

503 Paul VI, Discourse, November 21, 1964.
504 *LG* 57.
505 *LG* 58; cf. *Jn* 19:26-27.
511 *LG* 61.
515 *Lk* 1:48; Paul VI, *MC* 56.
516 *LG* 66.
517 Cf. Paul VI, *MC* 42; *SC* 103.
144 Lk 1:43; Jn 2:1; 19:25; cf. Mt 13:55; et al.
145 Council of Ephesus (431): DS 251.
160 LG 63; cf. Jn 19:26-27; Rom 8:29; Rev 12:17.

# Chapter V Reference
## Temptation & The Evil One

**538** The Gospels speak of a time of solitude for Jesus in the desert immediately after his baptism by John. Driven by the Spirit into the desert, Jesus remains there for forty days without eating; he lives among wild beasts, and angels minister to him.[241] At the end of this time Satan tempts him three times, seeking to compromise his filial attitude toward God. Jesus rebuffs these attacks, which recapitulate the temptations of Adam in Paradise and of Israel in the desert, and the devil leaves him "until an opportune time".[242]

**539** The evangelists indicate the salvific meaning of this mysterious event: Jesus is the new Adam who remained faithful just where the first Adam had given in to temptation. Jesus fulfills Israel's vocation perfectly: in contrast to those who had once provoked God during forty years in the desert, Christ reveals himself as God's Servant, totally obedient to the divine will. In this, Jesus is the devil's conqueror: he "binds the strong man" to take back his plunder.[243] Jesus' victory over the tempter in the desert anticipates victory at the Passion, the supreme act of obedience of his filial love for the Father.

**540** Jesus' temptation reveals the way in which the Son of God is Messiah, contrary to the way Satan proposes to him and the way men wish to attribute to him.[244] This is why Christ vanquished the Tempter for us: "For we have not a high priest who is unable to sympathize with our weaknesses, but one who in every respect has been tested as we are, yet without sinning."[245] By the solemn forty days of Lent the Church unites herself each year to the mystery of Jesus in the desert.

**566** The temptation in the desert shows Jesus, the humble Messiah, who triumphs over Satan by his total adherence to the plan of salvation willed by the Father.

**2725** Prayer is both a gift of grace and a determined response on our part. It always presupposes effort. The great figures of prayer of the Old Covenant before Christ, as well as the Mother of God, the saints, and he himself, all teach us this: prayer is a battle. Against whom? Against ourselves and against the wiles of the tempter who does all he can to turn man away from prayer, away from union with God. We pray as we live, because we live as we pray. If we do not want to act habitually according to the Spirit of Christ, neither can we pray habitually in his name. The "spiritual battle" of the Christian's new life is inseparable from the battle of prayer.

**2732** The most common yet most hidden temptation is our lack of faith. It expresses itself less by declared incredulity than by our actual preferences. When we begin to pray, a thousand labors or cares thought to be urgent vie for priority; once again, it is the moment of truth for the heart: what is its real love? Sometimes we turn to the Lord as a last resort, but do we really believe he is? Sometimes we enlist the Lord as an ally, but our heart remains presumptuous. In each case, our lack of faith reveals that we do not yet share in the disposition of a humble heart: "Apart from me, you can do nothing."[20]

**2733** Another temptation, to which presumption opens the gate, is acedia. The spiritual writers understand by this a form of depression due to lax ascetical practice, decreasing vigilance, carelessness of heart. "The spirit indeed is willing, but the flesh is weak."[21] The greater the height, the harder the fall. Painful as discouragement is, it is the reverse of presumption. The humble are not surprised by their distress; it leads them to trust more, to hold fast in constancy.

"Lead us not into temptation but deliver us from evil."

**2846** This petition goes to the root of the preceding one, for our sins result from our consenting to temptation; we therefore ask our Father not to "lead" us into temptation. It is difficult to translate the Greek verb used by a single English word: the Greek means both "do not allow us to enter into temptation" and "do not let us yield to temptation."[150] "God cannot be tempted by evil and he himself tempts no one";[151] on the contrary, he wants to set us free from evil. We ask him not to allow us to take the way that leads to sin. We are engaged in the battle "between flesh and spirit"; this petition implores the Spirit of discernment and strength.

**2847** The Holy Spirit makes us *discern* between trials, which are necessary for the growth of the inner man,[152] and temptation, which leads to sin and death.[153] We must also discern between being tempted and consenting to temptation. Finally, discernment unmasks the lie of temptation, whose object appears to be good, a "delight to the eyes" and desirable,[154] when in reality its fruit is death.

> God does not want to impose the good, but wants free beings. . . . There is a certain usefulness to temptation. No one but God knows what our soul has received from him, not even we ourselves. But temptation reveals it in order to teach us to know ourselves, and in this way we discover our evil inclinations and are obliged to give thanks for the goods that temptation has revealed to us.[155]

**2850** The last petition to our Father is also included in Jesus' prayer: "I am not asking you to take them out of the world, but I ask you to protect them from the evil one."[163] It touches each of us personally, but it is always "we" who pray, in communion with the whole Church, for the deliverance of the whole human family. The Lord's Prayer continually opens us to the range of God's economy of salvation. Our interdependence in the drama of sin and death is turned into solidarity in the Body of Christ, the "communion of saints."[164]

**2851** In this petition, evil is not an abstraction, but refers to a person, Satan, the Evil One, the angel who opposes God. The devil (dia-bolos) is the one who "throws himself across" God's plan and his work of salvation accomplished in Christ.

**2854** When we ask to be delivered from the Evil One, we pray as well to be freed from all evils, present, past, and future, of which he is the author or instigator. In this final petition, the Church brings before the Father all the distress of the world. Along with deliverance from the evils that overwhelm humanity, she implores the precious gift of peace and the grace of perseverance in expectation of Christ's return By praying in this way, she anticipates in humility of faith the gathering together of everyone and everything in him who has "the keys of Death and Hades," who "is and who was and who is to come, the Almighty."[174]

**391** Behind the disobedient choice of our first parents lurks a seductive voice, opposed to God, which makes them fall into death out of envy.[266] Scripture and the Church's Tradition see in this being a fallen angel, called "Satan" or the "devil".[267] The Church teaches that Satan was at first a good angel, made by God: "The devil and the other demons were indeed created naturally good by God, but they became evil by their own doing."[268]

**395** The power of Satan is, nonetheless, not infinite. He is only a creature, powerful from the fact that he is pure spirit, but still a creature. He cannot prevent the building up of God's reign. Although Satan may act in the world out of hatred for God and his kingdom in Christ Jesus, and although his action may cause grave injuries - of a spiritual nature and, indirectly, even of a physical nature- to each man and to society, the action is permitted by divine providence which with strength and gentleness guides human and cosmic history. It is a great mystery that providence should permit diabolical activity, but "we know that in everything God works for good with those who love him."[275]

**407** The doctrine of original sin, closely connected with that of redemption by Christ, provides lucid discernment of man's situation and activity in the world. By our first parents' sin, the devil has acquired a certain domination over man, even though man remains free. Original sin entails "captivity under the power of him who thenceforth had the power of death, that is, the devil".[298] Ignorance of the fact that man has a wounded nature inclined to evil gives rise to serious errors in the areas of education, politics, social action[299] and morals.

**409** This dramatic situation of "the whole world [which] is in the power of the evil one"[302] makes man's life a battle:

> The whole of man's history has been the story of dour combat with the powers of evil, stretching, so our Lord tells us, from the very dawn of history until the last day. Finding himself in the midst of the battle-field man has to struggle to do what is right, and it is at great cost to himself, and aided by God's grace, that he succeeds in achieving his own inner integrity.[303]

**1854** Sins are rightly evaluated according to their gravity. The distinction between mortal and venial sin, already evident in Scripture,[129] became part of the tradition of the Church. It is corroborated by human experience.

**1855** *Mortal sin* destroys charity in the heart of man by a grave violation of God's law; it turns man away from God, who is his ultimate end and his beatitude, by preferring an inferior good to him.
*Venial sin* allows charity to subsist, even though it offends and wounds it.

**1856** Mortal sin, by attacking the vital principle within us - that is, charity - necessitates a new initiative of God's mercy and a conversion of heart which is normally accomplished within the setting of the sacrament of reconciliation:

> When the will sets itself upon something that is of its nature incompatible with the charity that orients man toward his ultimate end, then the sin is mortal by its very object . . . whether it contradicts the love of God, such as blasphemy or perjury, or the love of neighbor, such as homicide or adultery. . . . But when the sinner's will is set upon something that of its nature involves a disorder, but is not opposed to the love of God and neighbor, such as thoughtless chatter or immoderate laughter and the like, such sins are venial.[130]

**1857** For a *sin* to be *mortal*, three conditions must together be met: "Mortal sin is sin whose object is grave matter and which is also committed with full knowledge and deliberate consent."[131]

**1868** Sin is a personal act. Moreover, we have a responsibility for the sins committed by others when we cooperate in them:
- by participating directly and voluntarily in them;
- by ordering, advising, praising, or approving them;
- by not disclosing or not hindering them when we have an obligation to do so;
- by protecting evil-doers.

**1869** Thus sin makes men accomplices of one another and causes concupiscence, violence, and injustice to reign among them. Sins give rise to social situations and institutions that are contrary to the divine goodness. "Structures of sin" are the expression and effect of personal sins. They lead their victims to do evil in their turn. In an analogous sense, they constitute a "social sin."[144]

241 Cf. Mk 1:12-13.
242 Lk 4:13.
243 Cf. Ps 95:10; Mk 3:27
244 Cf Mt 16:2 1-23.
245 Heb 4:15.
20 Jn 15:5.
21 Mt 26:41.
150 Cf. Mt 26:41.
151 Jas 113.
152 Cf. Lk 8:13-15; Acts 14:22; Rom 5:3-5; 2 Tim 3:12.
153 Cf. Jas 1:14-15.
154 Cf. Gen 3:6.
155 Origen, De orat. 29:PG 11,544CD.
163 Jn 17:15.
164 Cf. RP 16.
174 Rev 1:8,18; cf. Rev 1:4; Eph 1:10.
266 Cf. Gen 3:1-5; Wis 2:24.
267 Cf Jn 8:44; Rev 12:9.
268 Lateran Council IV (1215): DS 800.
275 Rom 8:28.
298 Council of Trent (1546): DS 1511; cf. Heb 2:14.
299 Cf. John Paul II, CA 25.
302 1 Jn 5:19; cf. 1 Pet 5:8.
303 GS 37 § 2.
129 Cf. 1 Jn 16-17.
130 St. Thomas Aquinas, STh I-II,88,2, corp. art.
131 RP 17 § 12.
144 John Paul II, RP 16.

# CHAPTER VI REFERENCE
## RECONCILIATION & FORGIVENESS

**978** "When we made our first profession of faith while receiving the holy Baptism that cleansed us, the forgiveness we received then was so full and complete that there remained in us absolutely nothing left to efface, neither original sin nor offenses committed by our own will, nor was there left any penalty to suffer in order to expiate them. . . . Yet the grace of Baptism delivers no one from all the weakness of nature. On the contrary, we must still combat the movements of concupiscence that never cease leading us into evil "[523]

**979** In this battle against our inclination towards evil, who could be brave and watchful enough to escape every wound of sin? "If the Church has the power to forgive sins, then Baptism cannot be her only means of using the keys of the Kingdom of heaven received from Jesus Christ. The Church must be able to forgive all penitents their offenses, even if they should sin until the last moment of their lives."[524]

**980** It is through the sacrament of Penance that the baptized can be reconciled with God and with the Church:

> Penance has rightly been called by the holy Fathers "a laborious kind of baptism." This sacrament of Penance is necessary for salvation for those who have fallen after Baptism, just as Baptism is necessary for salvation for those who have not yet been reborn.[525]

**1393** *Holy Communion separates us from sin.* The body of Christ we receive in Holy Communion is "given up for us," and the blood we drink "shed for the many for the forgiveness of sins." For this reason the Eucharist cannot unite us to Christ without at the same time cleansing us from past sins and preserving us from future sins:

For as often as we eat this bread and drink the cup, we proclaim the death of the Lord. If we proclaim the Lord's death, we proclaim the forgiveness of sins. If, as often as his blood is poured out, it is poured for the forgiveness of sins, I should always receive it, so that it may always forgive my sins. Because I always sin, I should always have a remedy.[230]

**1394** As bodily nourishment restores lost strength, so the Eucharist strengthens our charity, which tends to be weakened in daily life; and this living charity *wipes away venial sins*.[231] By giving himself to us Christ revives our love and enables us to break our disordered attachments to creatures and root ourselves in him:

**1422** "Those who approach the sacrament of Penance obtain pardon from God's mercy for the offense committed against him, and are, at the same time, reconciled with the Church which they have wounded by their sins and which by charity, by example, and by prayer labors for their conversion."[4]

**1423** It is called the sacrament of conversion because it makes sacramentally present Jesus' call to conversion, the first step in returning to the Father[5] from whom one has strayed by sin. It is called the sacrament of Penance, since it consecrates the Christian sinner's personal and ecclesial steps of conversion, penance, and satisfaction.

**1424** It is called the *sacrament of confession*, since the disclosure or confession of sins to a priest is an essential element of this sacrament. In a profound sense it is also a "confession" - acknowledgment and praise - of the holiness of God and of his mercy toward sinful man.
It is called the *sacrament of forgiveness*, since by the priest's sacramental absolution God grants the penitent "pardon and peace."[6]
It is called the *sacrament of Reconciliation*, because it imparts to the sinner the live of God who reconciles: "Be reconciled to God."[7] He who lives by God's merciful love is ready to respond to the Lord's call: "Go; first be reconciled to your brother."[8]

**1440** Sin is before all else an offense against God, a rupture of communion with him. At the same time it damages communion with the Church. For this reason conversion entails both God's forgiveness and reconciliation with the Church, which are expressed and accomplished liturgically by the sacrament of Penance and Reconciliation.

**1443** During his public life Jesus not only forgave sins, but also made plain the effect of this forgiveness: he reintegrated forgiven sinners into the community of the People of God from which sin had alienated or even excluded them. A remarkable sign of this is the fact that Jesus receives sinners at his table, a gesture that expresses in an astonishing way both God's forgiveness and the return to the bosom of the People of God.[44]

**1458** Without being strictly necessary, confession of everyday faults (venial sins) is nevertheless strongly recommended by the Church.[59] Indeed the regular confession of our venial sins helps us form our conscience, fight against evil tendencies, let ourselves be healed by Christ and progress in the life of the Spirit. By receiving more frequently through this sacrament the gift of the Father's mercy, we are spurred to be merciful as he is merciful:[60] Whoever confesses his sins . . . is already working with God. God indicts your sins; if you also indict them, you are joined with God. Man and sinner are, so to speak, two realities: when you hear "man" - this is what God has made; when you hear "sinner" - this is what man himself has made. Destroy what you have made, so that God may save what he has made. . . . When you begin to abhor what you have made, it is then that your good works are beginning, since you are accusing yourself of your evil works. The beginning of good works is the confession of evil works. You do the truth and come to the light.[61]

**1465** When he celebrates the sacrament of Penance, the priest is fulfilling the ministry of the Good Shepherd who seeks the lost sheep, of the Good Samaritan who binds up wounds, of the Father who awaits the prodigal son and welcomes him on his return, and of the just and impartial judge whose judgment is both just and merciful. The priest is the sign and the instrument of God's merciful love for the sinner.

**1466** The confessor is not the master of God's forgiveness, but its servant. The minister of this sacrament should unite himself to the intention and charity of Christ.[71] He should have a proven knowledge of Christian behavior, experience of human affairs, respect and sensitivity toward the one who has fallen; he must love the truth, be faithful to the Magisterium of the Church, and lead the penitent with patience toward healing and full maturity. He must pray and do penance for his penitent, entrusting him to the Lord's mercy.

**1468** "The whole power of the sacrament of Penance consists in restoring us to God's grace and joining us with him in an intimate friendship."[73] Reconciliation with God is thus the purpose and effect of this sacrament. For those who receive the sacrament of Penance with contrite heart and religious disposition, reconciliation "is usually followed by peace and serenity of conscience with strong spiritual consolation."[74] Indeed the sacrament of Reconciliation with God brings about a true "spiritual resurrection," restoration of the dignity and blessings of the life of the children of God, of which the most precious is friendship with God.[75]

**1469** This sacrament *reconciles us with the Church.* Sin damages or even breaks fraternal communion. The sacrament of Penance repairs or restores it. In this sense it does not simply heal the one restored to ecclesial communion, but has also a revitalizing effect on the life of the Church which suffered from the sin of one of her members.[76] Re-established or strengthened in the communion of saints, the sinner is made stronger by the exchange of spiritual goods among all the living members of the Body of Christ, whether still on pilgrimage or already in the heavenly homeland:[77]

523 Roman Catechism I, 11,3.
524 Roman Catechism I, 11,4.
525 Council Of Trent (1551): DS 1672; Cf. St. Gregory Of Nazianzus, Oratio 39,17:PG 36,356.
230 St. Ambrose, De Scar. 4,6,28:PL 16,446; cf. 1 Cor 11:26.

231 Cf. Council of Trent (1551): DS 1638.
4 LG 11 § 2.
5 Cf. Mk 1:15; Lk 15:18.
6 OP 46 formula of absolution.
7 2 Cor 5:20.
8 Mt 5:24.
44 Cf. Lk 15; 19:9.
59 Cf. Council of Trent: DS 1680; CIC, can. 988 § 2.
60 Cf. Lk 6:36.
61 St. Augustine, In Jo. ev. 12,13:PL 35,1491.
73 Roman Catechism, II,V,18.
74 Council of Trent (1551): DS 1674.
75 Cf. Lk 15:32.
76 Cf. 1 Cor 12:26.
77 Cf. LG 48-50.

# CHAPTER VII REFERENCE
## LEADERSHIP & STEWARDSHIP

**459** The Word became flesh to be our model of holiness: "Take my yoke upon you, and learn from me." "I am the way, and the truth, and the life; no one comes to the Father, but by me."[74] On the mountain of the Transfiguration, the Father commands: "Listen to him!"[75] Jesus is the model for the Beatitudes and the norm of the new law: "Love one another as I have loved you."[76] This love implies an effective offering of oneself, after his example.[77]

**871** "The Christian faithful are those who, inasmuch as they have been incorporated in Christ through Baptism, have been constituted as the people of God; for this reason, since they have become sharers in Christ's priestly, prophetic, and royal office in their own manner, they are called to exercise the mission which God has entrusted to the Church to fulfill in the world, in accord with the condition proper to each one."[385]

**873** The very differences which the Lord has willed to put between the members of his body serve its unity and mission. For "in the Church there is diversity of ministry but unity of mission. To the apostles and their successors Christ has entrusted the office of teaching, sanctifying and governing in his name and by his power. But the laity are made to share in the priestly, prophetical, and kingly office of Christ; they have therefore, in the Church and in the world, their own assignment in the mission of the whole People of God."[387] Finally, "from both groups [hierarchy and laity] there exist Christian faithful who are consecrated to God in their own special manner and serve the salvific mission of the Church through the profession of the evangelical counsels."[388]

**904** "Christ . . . fulfills this prophetic office, not only by the hierarchy . . . but also by the laity. He accordingly both establishes them as witnesses and provides them with the sense of the faith [sensus fidei] and the grace of the word"[438] To teach in order to lead others to faith is the task of every preacher and of each believer.[439]

**935** To proclaim the faith and to plant his reign, Christ sends his apostles and their successors. He gives them a share in his own mission. From him they receive the power to act in his person.

**941** Lay people share in Christ's priesthood: ever more united with him, they exhibit the grace of Baptism and Confirmation in all dimensions of their personal family, social and ecclesial lives, and so fulfill the call to holiness addressed to all the baptized.

**942** By virtue of their prophetic mission, lay people "are called . . . to be witnesses to Christ in all circumstances and at the very heart of the community of mankind" (GS 43 § 4).

**945** Already destined for him through Baptism, the person who surrenders himself to the God he loves above all else thereby consecrates himself more intimately to God's service and to the good of the whole Church.

**516** Christ's whole earthly life - his words and deeds, his silences and sufferings, indeed his manner of being and speaking - is Revelation of the Father. Jesus can say: "Whoever has seen me has seen the Father", and the Father can say: "This is my Son, my Chosen; listen to him!"[177] Because our Lord became man in order to do his Father's will, even the least characteristics of his mysteries manifest "God's love. . . among us".[178]

**520** In all of his life Jesus presents himself as our model. He is "the perfect man",[191] who invites us to become his disciples and follow him. In humbling himself, he has given us an example to imitate, through his prayer he draws us to pray, and by his poverty he calls us to accept freely the privation and persecutions that may come our way.[192]

**561** "The whole of Christ's life was a continual teaching: his silences, his miracles, his gestures, his prayer, his love for people, his special affection for the little and the poor, his acceptance of the total sacrifice on the Cross for the redemption of the world, and his Resurrection are the actualization of his word and the fulfillment of Revelation" John Paul II, CT 9).

**562** Christ's disciples are to conform themselves to him until he is formed in them (cf. Gal 4:19). "For this reason we, who have been made like to him, who have died with him and risen with him, are taken up into the mysteries of his life, until we reign together with him" (LG 7 § 4).

**564** By his obedience to Mary and Joseph, as well as by his humble work during the long years in Nazareth, Jesus gives us the example of holiness in the daily life of family and work.

**565** From the beginning of his public life, at his baptism, Jesus is the "Servant", wholly consecrated to the redemptive work that he will accomplish by the "baptism" of his Passion.

**60** After agreeing to baptize him along with the sinners, John the Baptist looked at Jesus and pointed him out as the "Lamb of God, who takes away the sin of the wÀrld".[422] By doing so, he reveals that Jesus is at the same time the suffering Servant who silently allows himself to be led to the slaughter and who bears the sin of the multitudes, and also the Paschal Lamb, the symbol of Israel's redemption at the first Passover.[423] Christ's whole life expresses his mission: "to serve, and to give his life as a ransom for many."[424]

**2427** Human work proceeds directly from persons created in the image of God and called to prolong the work of creation by subduing the earth, both with and for one another.[210] Hence work is a duty: "If any one will not work, let him not eat."[211] Work honors the Creator's gifts and the talents received from him. It can also be redemptive. By enduring the hardship of work[212] in union with Jesus, the carpenter of Nazareth and the one crucified on Calvary, man collaborates in a certain fashion with the Son of God in his redemptive work. He shows himself to be a disciple of Christ by carrying the cross, daily, in the work he is called to accomplish.[213] Work can be a means of sanctification and a way of animating earthly realities with the Spirit of Christ.

**2432** Those responsible for business enterprises are responsible to society for the economic and ecological effects of their operations.[218] They have an obligation to consider the good of persons and not only the increase of profits. Profits are necessary, however. They make possible the investments that ensure the future of a business and they guarantee employment.

**1820** Christian hope unfolds from the beginning of Jesus' preaching in the proclamation of the beatitudes. The beatitudes raise our hope toward heaven as the new Promised Land; they trace the path that leads through the trials that await the disciples of Jesus. But through the merits of Jesus Christ and of his Passion, God keeps us in the "hope that does not disappoint."[88] Hope is the "sure and steadfast anchor of the soul . . . that enters . . . where Jesus has gone as a forerunner on our behalf."[89] Hope is also a weapon that protects us in the struggle of salvation: "Let us . . . put on the breastplate of faith and charity, and for a helmet the hope of salvation."[90] It affords us joy even under trial: "Rejoice in your hope, be patient in tribulation."[91] Hope is expressed and nourished in prayer, especially in the Our Father, the summary of everything that hope leads us to desire.

74 Mt 11:29; Jn 14:6.
75 Mk 9:7; cf. Dt 6:4-5.
76 Jn 15:12.
77 Cf. Mk 8:34.
385 CIC, Can. 204 para 1; Cf. LG 31.
386 CIC, Can. 208; Cf. LG 32.
387 AA 2.
388 CIC, Can. 207 § 2.
438 LG 35.
439 St. Thomas Aquinas, STh. III,71,4 ad 3.
177 Jn 14:9; Lk 9:35; cf. Mt 17:5; Mk 9:7 ("my beloved Son").
178 1 Jn 4:9.
191 GS 38; cf. Rom 1 5:5; Phil 2:5.
192 Cf. Jn 13:15; Lk 11:1; Mt 5:11-12.
419 Jn 12:27.

420 Jn 18:11.
421 Jn 19:30; 19:28.
422 Jn 1:29; cf. Lk 3:21; Mt 3:14-15; Jn 1:36.
423 Isa 53:7,12; cf. Jer 11:19; Ex 12:3-14; Jn 19:36; 1 Cor 5:7.
424 Mk 10:45.
210 Cf. Gen 1:28; GS 34; CA 31.
211 2 Thess 3:10; Cf. 1 Thess 4:11.
212 Cf. Gen 3:14-19.
213 Cf. LE 27.
218 Cf. CA 37.
88 Rom 5:5.
89 Heb 6:19-20.
90 1 Thess 5:8.
91 Rom 12:12.

# CHAPTER VIII REFERENCE
## IMAGE OF CHRIST & HUMANITY

**1397** *The Eucharist commits us to the poor.* To receive in truth the Body and Blood of Christ given up for us, we must recognize Christ in the poorest, his brethren:
You have tasted the Blood of the Lord, yet you do not recognize your brother,. . . . You dishonor this table when you do not judge worthy of sharing your food someone judged worthy to take part in this meal. . . . God freed you from all your sins and invited you here, but you have not become more merciful.[236]

**1398** *The Eucharist and the unity of Christians.* Before the greatness of this mystery St. Augustine exclaims, *"O sacrament of devotion! O sign of unity! O bond of charity!"*[237] The more painful the experience of the divisions in the Church which break the common participation in the table of the Lord, the more urgent are our prayers to the Lord that the time of complete unity among all who believe in him may return.

**1944** Respect for the human person considers the other "another self." It presupposes respect for the fundamental rights that flow from the dignity intrinsic of the person.

**1945** The equality of men concerns their dignity as persons and the rights that flow from it.

**1946** The differences among persons belong to God's plan, who wills that we should need one another. These differences should encourage charity.

**2392** "Love is the fundamental and innate vocation of every human being" (FC 11).

236 St. John Chrysostom, *Hom. in 1 Cor.* 27,4:PG 61,229-230; cf. *Mt* 25:40.
237 St. Augustine, *In Jo. ev.* 26,13:PL 35,1613; cf. *SC* 47.

# Chapter IX Reference
## The Passion

**599** Jesus' violent death was not the result of chance in an unfortunate coincidence of circumstances, but is part of the mystery of God's plan, as St. Peter explains to the Jews of Jerusalem in his first sermon on Pentecost: "This Jesus [was] delivered up according to the definite plan and foreknowledge of God."[393] This Biblical language does not mean that those who handed him over were merely passive players in a scenario written in advance by God.[394]

**601** The Scriptures had foretold this divine plan of salvation through the putting to death of "the righteous one, my Servant" as a mystery of universal redemption, that is, as the ransom that would free men from the slavery of sin.[397] Citing a confession of faith that he himself had "received", St. Paul professes that "Christ died for our sins in accordance with the scriptures."[398] In particular Jesus' redemptive death fulfills Isaiah's prophecy of the suffering Servant.[399] Indeed Jesus himself explained the meaning of his life and death in the light of God's suffering Servant.[400] After his Resurrection he gave this interpretation of the Scriptures to the disciples at Emmaus, and then to the apostles.[401]

**610** Jesus gave the supreme expression of his free offering of himself at the meal shared with the twelve Apostles "on the night he was betrayed".[429] On the eve of his Passion, while still free, Jesus transformed this Last Supper with the apostles into the memorial of his voluntary offering to the Father for the salvation of men: "This is my body which is given for you." "This is my blood of the covenant, which is poured out for many for the forgiveness of sins."[430]

**611** The Eucharist that Christ institutes at that moment will be the memorial of his sacrifice.[431] Jesus includes the apostles in his own offering and bids them perpetuate it.[432] By doing so, the

Lord institutes his apostles as priests of the New Covenant: "For their sakes I sanctify myself, so that they also may be sanctified in truth."433

**612** The cup of the New Covenant, which Jesus anticipated when he offered himself at the Last Supper, is afterwards accepted by him from his Father's hands in his agony in the garden at Gethsemani,434 making himself "obedient unto death". Jesus prays: "My Father, if it be possible, let this cup pass from me. . ."435 Thus he expresses the horror that death represented for his human nature. Like ours, his human nature is destined for eternal life; but unlike ours, it is perfectly exempt from sin, the cause of death.436 Above all, his human nature has been assumed by the divine person of the "Author of life", the "Living One".437 By accepting in his human will that the Father's will be done, he accepts his death as redemptive, for "he himself bore our sins in his body on the tree."438

Christ's death is the unique and definitive sacrifice

**613** Christ's death is both the *Paschal sacrifice* that accomplishes the definitive redemption of men, through "the Lamb of God, who takes away the sin of the world",439 and the *sacrifice of the New Covenant*, which restores man to communion with God by reconciling him to God through the "blood of the covenant, which was poured out for many for the forgiveness of sins".440

**615** "For as by one man's disobedience many were made sinners, so by one man's obedience many will be made righteous."443 By his obedience unto death, Jesus accomplished the substitution of the suffering Servant, who "makes himself an *offering for sin*", when "he bore the sin of many", and who "shall make many to be accounted righteous", for "he shall bear their iniquities".444 Jesus atoned for our faults and made satisfaction for our sins to the Father.445 Jesus consummates his sacrifice on the cross

**616** It is love "to the end"446 that confers on Christ's sacrifice its value as redemption and reparation, as atonement and satisfaction. He knew and loved us all when he offered his life.447 Now "the love of Christ controls us, because we are convinced that one has died for all; therefore all have died."[448] No man, not even the holiest, was ever able to take on himself the sins of all men and offer himself as a sacrifice for all. The existence in Christ of the divine person of the Son, who at once surpasses and embraces all human persons, and constitutes himself as the Head of all mankind, makes possible his redemptive sacrifice for all.

**618** The cross is the unique sacrifice of Christ, the "one mediator between God and men".[452] But because in his incarnate divine person he has in some way united himself to every man, "the possibility of being made partners, in a way known to God, in the paschal mystery" is offered to all men.[453] He calls his disciples to "take up [their] cross and follow [him]",[454] for "Christ also suffered for [us], leaving [us] an example so that [we] should follow in his steps."[455] In fact Jesus desires to associate with his redeeming sacrifice those who were to be its first beneficiaries.[456] This is achieved supremely in the case of his mother, who was associated more intimately than any other person in the mystery of his redemptive suffering.[457]

> Apart from the cross there is no other ladder by which we may get to heaven.[458]

**621** Jesus freely offered himself for our salvation. Beforehand, during the Last Supper, he both symbolized this offering and made it really present: "This is my body which is given for you"[1]

**623** By his loving obedience to the Father, "unto death, even death on a cross" (*Phil* 2:8), Jesus fulfills the atoning mission (cf. *Is* 53:10) of the suffering Servant, who will "make many righteous; and he shall bear their iniquities" (*Is* 53:11; cf. *Rom* 5:19).

**1344** Thus from celebration to celebration, as they proclaim the Paschal mystery of Jesus "until he comes," the pilgrim People of God advances, "following the narrow way of the cross,"[170] toward the heavenly banquet, when all the elect will be seated at the table of the kingdom.

**1365** Because it is the memorial of Christ's Passover, the Eucharist is also a sacrifice. The sacrificial character of the Eucharist is manifested in the very words of institution: "This is my body which is given for you" and "This cup which is poured out for you is the New Covenant in my blood."[187] In the Eucharist Christ gives us the very body which he gave up for us on the cross, the very blood which he "poured out for many for the forgiveness of sins."[188]

393 Acts 2:23.
394 Cf. Acts 3:13.
397 Isa 53:11; cf. 53:12; Jn 8:34-36; Acts 3:14.
398 1 Cor 15:3; cf. also Acts 3:18; 7:52; 13:29; 26:22-23.
399 Cf. Isa 53:7-8 and Acts 8:32-35.
400 Cf. Mt 20:28.
401 Cf. Lk 24:25-27, 44-45.429 Roman Missal, EP 111; cf. Mt 26:20; 1 Cor 11:23.
429 Roman Missal, EP 111; cf. Mt 26:20; 1 Cor 11:23.
430 Lk 22:19; Mt 26:28; cf. 1 Cor 5:7.
431 1 Cor 11:25.
432 Cf. Lk 22:19.
433 Jn 17:19; cf. Council of Trent: DS 1752; 1764.
434 Cf. Mt 26:42; Lk 22:20.
435 Phil 2:8; Mt 26:39; cf. Heb 5:7-8.
436 Cf. Rom 5:12; Heb 4:15.
437 Cf. Acts 3:15; Rev 1:17; Jn 1:4; 5:26.
438 1 Pet 224; cf. Mt 26:42.
439 Jn 1:29; cf. 8:34-36; 1 Cor 5:7; 1 Pet 1:19.
440 Mt 26:28; cf. Ex 24:8; Lev 16:15-16; 1 Cor 11:25.
443 Rom 5:19.
444 Isa 53:10-12.
445 Cf. Council of Trent (1547): DS 1529.
446 Jn 13:1.
447 Cf. Gal 2:20; Eph 5:2, 25.
448 2 Cor 5:14.
452 1 Tim 2:5.
453 GS 22 § 5; cf. § 2.
454 Mt 16:24.
455 1 Pet 2:21.
456 Cf Mk 10:39; Jn 21:18-19; Col 1:24.
457 Cf. Lk 2:35.
458 St. Rose of Lima, cf. P. Hansen, Vita mirabilis (Louvain, 1668).
1 (Lk 22:19).
170 AG 1; cf. 1 Cor 11:26.
187 Lk 22:19-20.
188 Mt 26:28.

# CHAPTER X REFERENCE
## RESURRECTION & HOPE

**639** The mystery of Christ's resurrection is a real event, with manifestations that were historically verified, as the New Testament bears witness. In about A.D. 56 St. Paul could already write to the Corinthians: "I delivered to you as of first importance what I also received, that Christ died for our sins in accordance with the scriptures, and that he was buried, that he was raised on the third day in accordance with the scriptures, and that he appeared to Cephas, then to the Twelve. . ."[491] The Apostle speaks here of the living tradition of the Resurrection which he had learned after his conversion at the gates of Damascus.[492]

**651** "If Christ has not been raised, then our preaching is in vain and your faith is in vain."[521] The Resurrection above all constitutes the confirmation of all Christ's works and teachings. All truths, even those most inaccessible to human reason, find their justification if Christ by his Resurrection has given the definitive proof of his divine authority, which he had promised.

**653** The truth of Jesus' divinity is confirmed by his Resurrection. He had said: "When you have lifted up the Son of man, then you will know that I am he."[524] The Resurrection of the crucified one shows that he was truly "I AM", the Son of God and God himself. So St. Paul could declare to the Jews: "What God promised to the fathers, this he has fulfilled to us their children by raising Jesus; as also it is written in the second psalm, 'You are my Son, today I have begotten you.'"[525] Christ's Resurrection is closely linked to the Incarnation of God's Son, and is its fulfillment in accordance with God's eternal plan.

**654** The Paschal mystery has two aspects: by his death, Christ liberates us from sin; by his Resurrection, he opens for us the way to a new life. This new life is above all justification that reinstates us in God's grace, "so that as Christ was raised from the dead by the glory of the Father, we too might walk in newness of life."[526] Justification consists in both victory over the death caused by sin and a new participation in grace.[527] It brings about filial adoption so that men become Christ's brethren, as Jesus himself called his disciples after his Resurrection: "Go and tell my brethren."[528] We are brethren not by nature, but by the gift of grace, because that adoptive filiation gains us a real share in the life of the only Son, which was fully revealed in his Resurrection.

**656** Faith in the Resurrection has as its object an event which as historically attested to by the disciples, who really encountered the Risen One. At the same time, this event is mysteriously transcendent insofar as it is the entry of Christ's humanity into the glory of God.

**657** The empty tomb and the linen cloths lying there signify in themselves that by God's power Christ's body had escaped the bonds of death and corruption. They prepared the disciples to encounter the Risen Lord.

**995** To be a witness to Christ is to be a "witness to his Resurrection," to "[have eaten and drunk] with him after he rose from the dead."[549] Encounters with the risen Christ characterize the Christian hope of resurrection. We shall rise like Christ, with him, and through him.

**1002** Christ will raise us up "on the last day"; but it is also true that, in a certain way, we have already risen with Christ. For, by virtue of the Holy Spirit, Christian life is already now on earth a participation in the death and Resurrection of Christ:
And you were buried with him in Baptism, in which you were also raised with him through faith in the working of God, who raised him from the dead . . . . If then you have been raised with Christ, seek the things that are above, where Christ is, seated at the right hand of God.[559]

**1003** United with Christ by Baptism, believers already truly participate in the heavenly life of the risen Christ, but this life remains "hidden with Christ in God."[560] The Father has already "raised us up with him, and made us sit with him in the heavenly places in Christ Jesus."[561] Nourished with his body in the Eucharist, we already belong to the Body of Christ. When we rise on the last day we "also will appear with him in glory."[562]

**1347** Is this not the same movement as the Paschal meal of the risen Jesus with his disciples? Walking with them he explained the Scriptures to them; sitting with them at table "he took bread, blessed and broke it, and gave it to them."[174]

**1392** What material food produces in our bodily life, Holy Communion wonderfully achieves in our spiritual life. Communion with the flesh of the risen Christ, a flesh "given life and giving life through the Holy Spirit,"[229]preserves, increases, and renews the life of grace received at Baptism. This growth in Christian life needs the nourishment of Eucharistic Communion, the bread for our pilgrimage until the moment of death, when it will be given to us as viaticum.

**1405** There is no surer pledge or dearer sign of this great hope in the new heavens and new earth "in which righteousness dwells,"[248] than the Eucharist. Every time this mystery is celebrated, "the work of our redemption is carried on" and we "break the one bread that provides the medicine of immortality, the antidote for death, and the food that makes us live forever in Jesus Christ."[249]

**1818** The virtue of hope responds to the aspiration to happiness which God has placed in the heart of every man; it takes up the hopes that inspire men's activities and purifies them so as to order them to the Kingdom of heaven; it keeps man from discouragement; it sustains him during times of abandonment; it opens up his heart in expectation of eternal beatitude. Buoyed up by hope, he is preserved from selfishness and led to the happiness that flows from charity.

**1821** We can therefore hope in the glory of heaven promised by

God to those who love him and do his will.[92] In every circumstance, each one of us should hope, with the grace of God, to persevere "to the end"[93] and to obtain the joy of heaven, as God's eternal reward for the good works accomplished with the grace of Christ. In hope, the Church prays for "all men to be saved."[94] She longs to be united with Christ, her Bridegroom, in the glory of heaven:

> Hope, O my soul, hope. You know neither the day nor the hour. Watch carefully, for everything passes quickly, even though your impatience makes doubtful what is certain, and turns a very short time into a long one. Dream that the more you struggle, the more you prove the love that you bear your God, and the more you will rejoice one day with your Beloved, in a happiness and rapture that can never end.[95]

491 1 Cor 15:3-4.
492 Cf. Acts 9:3-18.
521 1 Cor 15:14.
524 Jn 8:28.
525 Acts 13:32-33; cf. Ps 2:7.
526 Rom 6:4; cf. 4:25.
527 Cf. Eph 2:4-5; 1 Pet 1:3.
528 Mt 28:10; Jn 20:17.
549 Acts 1:22; 10:41; cf. 4:33.
559 Col 2:12; 3:1.
560 Col 3:3; cf. Phil 3:20.
561 Eph 2:6.
562 Col 3:4.
174 Cf. Lk 24:13-35.
229 PO 5.
248 2 Pet 3:13.
249 LG 3; St. Ignatius of Antioch, Ad Eph. 20,2:SCh 10,76.
95 St. Teresa of Avila, Excl. 15:3.

# "WHO DO YOU SAY I AM?" REFERENCE
## THE NAME OF JESUS

**452** The name Jesus means "God saves". The child born of the Virgin Mary is called Jesus, "for he will save his people from their sins" (Mt 1:21): "there is no other name under heaven given among men by which we must be saved" (Acts 4:12).

**453** The title "Christ" means "Anointed One" (Messiah). Jesus is the Christ, for "God anointed Jesus of Nazareth with the Holy Spirit and with power" (Acts 10:38). He was the one "who is to come" (Lk 7:19), the object of "the hope of Israel" (Acts 28:20).

**454** The title "Son of God" signifies the unique and eternal relationship of Jesus Christ to God his Father: he is the only Son of the Father (cf. Jn 1:14, 18; 3:16, 18); he is God himself (cf. Jn 1:1). To be a Christian, one must believe that Jesus Christ is the Son of God (cf. Acts 8:37; 1 Jn 2:23).

**455** The title "Lord" indicates divine sovereignty. To confess or invoke Jesus as Lord is to believe in his divinity. "No one can say 'Jesus is Lord' except by the Holy Spirit'" (1 Cor 12:3).

# ABOUT THE AUTHOR

**G**reg **Wasinski** is a full time Catholic Christian Inspirational Speaker and Author. Greg's message of faith and real life is delivered in a genuine and attainable way. His easy to understand style helps people desire a deeper relationship with God while finding the real life application of their Catholic faith to encounter the person of Jesus Christ in the world.

As a presenter, he offers family workshops, intergenerational parish missions, men's conference keynotes, staff/volunteer team building development and Confirmation retreats across the country. Greg is also heard as a regular radio contributor and guest on many shows across the country including his own featured segments on *The Catholic Channel on Sirius XM Radio*. Ultimately, it's his passion to meet his audience where they are on their faith journey and provide support to Pastors, parish staff and ministry leaders as they continue to deepen faith formation for their communities. He exemplifies a true care for our church's future by opening up dialogue that reminds us why we believe what we believe.

Prior to answering his call into ministry and founding "Let Me Be..." Ministries, Greg successfully held a career as a corporate executive. His ministry is identified nationally by its signature "bee" logo as a reminder to "Be nothing more than God created you to be." Greg holds a certificate of Scriptural Theology from John Paul the Great Catholic University, in Escondido, CA. He is married to Aimee and they reside in Chagrin Falls, OH with their two children and two German Shepherds.

For more information, visit: www.Wasinski.com

# CONTACT INFORMATION

LMBM Inc.
8584 B  East Washington St.
#108
Chagrin Falls, OH 44023

www.LMBMInc.org

www.FaithandRealLife.com

*LMBM Inc. is a registered 501(c)3  non-profit corporation. If you would like to support the ongoing efforts of the ministry, please send donations to the address above or contributions are accepted online at www.LMBMInc.org*

# ALSO AVAILABLE:

"Let Me Be..."
Ministries

**"All I Ever Have to Be..."** Audio CD is a combination of songs featuring the beautiful vocals of Aimee Wasinski, and the authentically genuine reflections of Inspirational Speaker and Author, Greg Wasinski. You'll be sure to find yourself lost in the message to simply be who God created you to be. Perfect to share with family, friends and members of your faith community.

This product can be ordered in bulk for a discounted price. Inquire for details.

**www.FaithandRealLife.com**

# ALSO AVAILABLE:

"Let Me Be..."
Ministries

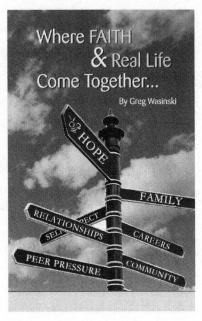

**"Where Faith & Real Life Come Together..."** is a faith-filled inspirational book about the discovery to recognize all the ways faith plays out in the world around us. This compilation of stories, coupled with reflection questions, will help you notice how God is at work every day. No matter where you are on your faith journey, you will be sure to find a relation to your own life on the pages within.

This product can be ordered in bulk for a discounted price. Inquire for details.

## www.FaithandRealLife.com

Made in the USA
Middletown, DE
18 February 2016